FINLAND

Helsinki

Leningrad

Sea

Tallinn
ESTONIA

Riga
LATVIA

LITHUANIA
Kovno
Vilna

EAST
RUSSIA

Minsk

Moscow

Tula

SOVIET UNION

Warsaw

POLAND UNDER
GERMAN RULE

Cracow

Lvov

TRANSNISTRIA

Kiev

UKRAINE

Kharkov

Stalingrad

Rostov

Grozny

Caspian Sea

IA

Budapest

HUNGARY

ANAT

RUMANIA

Bucharest

Belgrade

SERBIA

Sofia

BULGARIA

CRIMEA

Black Sea

Istanbul

Ankara

GREECE

TURKEY

Athens

Crete

Cyprus

Sea

The German Reich

Areas under German Administration
and Occupation

German satellites

Italy and annexed areas

0   100   200   300

Miles

Books by Milton Meltzer

WORLD OF OUR FATHERS
The Jews of Eastern Europe

REMEMBER THE DAYS
A Short History of the Jewish American

BOUND FOR THE RIO GRANDE
The Mexican Struggle, 1845–1850

SLAVERY
From the Rise of Western Civilization to Today (2 volumes)

A PICTORIAL HISTORY OF BLACKAMERICANS
(with Langston Hughes and C. Eric Lincoln)

THE EYE OF CONSCIENCE
Photographers and Social Change

LANGSTON HUGHES
A Biography

UNDERGROUND MAN
A Novel

THE RIGHT TO REMAIN SILENT

NEVER TO FORGET

The Jews of the Holocaust

MILTON MELTZER

HARPER & ROW, PUBLISHERS

ACKNOWLEDGMENTS

I gratefully acknowledge support from the Anti-Defamation League
of B'nai B'rith, which aided in my research for this book. I am also
indebted to the YIVO Institute for Jewish Research and its librarians,
Dina Abramowicz and Bella Weinberg, whose help was indispensable
to the writing of this book.

Acknowledgment is made for permission to quote from the following works:
Fromm, Bella, *Blood and Banquets*, copyright 1942 by Cooperation Publishing Co.,
Inc. Reprinted by permission of Harper & Row, Publishers, Inc. Shirer, William
L., *Berlin Diary*, copyright 1941 by William L. Shirer. Reprinted by permission
of Alfred A. Knopf, Inc. Fackenheim, Emil L., "Torture Through Senseless
System," *Midstream*, April 1975. Letter by David Buffum from Henry Zieger,
The Case Against Adolf Eichmann, copyright © 1960 by Henry Zieger. Reprinted
by arrangement with The New American Library, Inc., New York, N.Y. Libau,
M. I., "That Bloody Day in November," *Congress Weekly*, vol. 9, no. 34, November
13, 1942. Dworzecki, Mark, "A Day in the Vilna Ghetto," *Jewish Frontier*,
May 1952. Passages by Levi Shalit, Shaye Gertner, Reuben Rosenberg, and
Stanislaw Kohn, and the record of a meeting held in February 1943 by the
Hechalutz, Bialystok Branch, all from *Anthology of Holocaust Literature*, edited
by Jacob Glatstein et al. Copyright © 1968 by The Jewish Publication Society of
America. Reprinted by permission of The Jewish Publication Society of America.
Ringelblum, Emmanuel, *Notes from the Warsaw Ghetto: The Journal of Emmanuel
Ringelblum*, translated from the Yiddish and edited by Jacob Sloan, copyright
© 1958. Used with permission of McGraw-Hill Book Company. Passages by
Georges Wellers, W. Szpilman, Johann Kremer, and Ludwik Hirszfeld from
Gerhard Schoenberner, *The Yellow Star: The Persecution of the Jews in Europe,
1933–1945*. Original German edition, *Der Gelbe Stern*, copyright © 1960 by Gerhard
Schoenberner. Revised edition copyright © 1969 by Gerhard Schoenberner.
English translation copyright © 1969 by Transworld Publishers, Ltd. Reprinted by
permission of Bantam Books, Inc. Passage by Hans Baermann from Eugen Kogon,
*The Theory and Practice of Hell: The German Concentration Camps and the
System Behind Them*, copyright 1950 by Octagon Books. Reprinted by permission
of Farrar, Straus & Giroux, Inc. Kaplan, Chaim, *Scroll of Agony*, edited and
translated by Abraham Katsh, copyright © 1963 by Abraham Katsh. Reprinted by
permission of Macmillan Publishing Co., Inc. Passage by Jeanette Wolf from
We Survived, edited by Eric Boehm, copyright © 1966, Clio Press, Santa Barbara,
Calif. Reprinted by permission of Eric Boehm. Passages by Feigele Wladka and

In Memory of Max Hahn

CONTENTS

NEVER
TO FORGET

Why Remember?

I was fifteen years old when I first noticed the strange words "Nazi" and "Hitler" in the newspaper. I lived in Worcester, a city in the center of Massachusetts. It was September 1930, and I was just starting my junior year in high school. I used to read the papers, but not very thoroughly. Sports, the funnies, stories about local people, rarely any foreign news.

But on this day something caught my eye in a report datelined from Germany. A hundred-odd members of Adolf Hitler's Nazi party had just been elected to the German legislature—the Reichstag they called it—and they had shown up for the first session wearing brown uniforms and shouting, "Deutschland erwache! Jude verrecke!"

The paper obligingly explained what those foreign words meant: Germany awake! Jew perish!

Who was Hitler? What was a Nazi? Did the Germans take that slogan seriously—"Jew perish!"

It was those words that had leaped out at me from the small print. I wasn't looking for them; I didn't know they would be there. Still, I saw them as with a special sense, attuned to those three letters, J-E-W. The same sudden alarm would go off in a busy place—the school gym, the Y swimming pool, the corner hangout—if the word "Jew" were spoken by someone in the crowd. Through the confusion of noise the sound would arrow straight into my brain.

I was Jewish, of course, but a feeble kind of Jew, as I think of it now. I mean I had no religious training and almost no knowledge of Jewish life, history, or language. Our neighborhood was very mixed, and so were the schools I went to. I thought of myself as an American. If someone said yes, but what *kind* of American, then I'd say Jewish. Once on a Saturday morning an old Jewish widow who had just moved into the neighborhood saw me on the street and asked me to come into her house and light the stove. I wondered why she couldn't light it herself, but I did it, and she gave me a cookie. When I told my mother about it, she laughed and said, "She took you for a *Shabbos goy.*" She explained that religious Jews could not light a fire on the Sabbath. If they needed it, they'd ask a non-Jew, a goy, to do it.

I thought it was funny, too.

Then why did my skin prickle when I saw those words in the newspaper? Whatever kind of Jew I was, I had somehow absorbed the knowledge that Jews lived under threat. I had heard of the Jews of Egypt, enslaved under Pharaoh, and of how Haman's plan to annihilate the Jews of Persia had been foiled by Queen Esther. I knew vaguely about the persecution of the Jews during the Crusades and that the Inquisition had driven the Jews from Spain. Somewhere I had seen the word "pogrom" in print, knew it meant bloody riots against the Jews, and linked it to the immigrants who, like my mother and father, had fled Eastern Europe. On the street I had heard Jewish boys called "kike" and seen them fling themselves upon their tormentors.

But for politicians to stand up now in public and shout that the Jews must die?

I shuddered. "That could never happen here, could it, Pa?" He looked up, then smiled to reassure me. "Don't worry about it," he said. "Hitler and those Nazis of his—they won't last long."

They didn't. Not in the long perspective of time. They took power in 1933; they lost power in 1945. Twelve years. It's the length of time most of us spend in grade school and high school. That's only about a sixth of the average life span.

But how do you measure the cost of those dozen years of Nazi rule over Germany and most of Europe? By the time Hitler's power was smashed, 29 million people were dead. They were from many different countries, including Hitler's Germany and our United States.

Among the myriad slaughtered were the Jews. Six million of them. Two out of every three in Europe. One-third of the world's Jews. Statistics. But each was a man, a woman, or a child. Each had a name. Each suffered his or her own death.

Historians now speak of Hitler's extermination of the Jews as the Holocaust. The word derives from the word *olah* in the Hebrew Bible. It had the religious meaning of a burnt sacrifice. In the Greek translation of the Old Testament the word became *holokauston*. The English definition made it "an offering wholly consumed by fire." In our century it has acquired the secular meaning of a general disaster. But what Hitler did added another meaning to the dictionary definition: "a complete or thorough sacrifice or destruction, especially by fire, as of large numbers of human beings." (The Hebrew noun the Israelis use for it is *Shoa*. In Yiddish the word is *Khurbn*.)

The Holocaust was one of innumerable crimes committed by the Nazis. Then why single out the extermination of the Jews? Is it necessary to remember? Is it good? Can it even be understood by those who have come after?

No one would claim that the Nazi extermination of the Jews was greater or more tragic than what has been done to other persecuted peoples. Such comparisons are unfeeling and fruitless. What is historically significant is its uniqueness. There is no precedent for it in Jewish history. Nor in the history of any other people.

Civilians in the past have been massacred for what men called "reasonable" goals, utilitarian goals—to extend power, to acquire wealth, to increase territory, to stamp out opposition, to force conversion. What some power conceived to be in its self-interest was the reason behind the persecution.

But Hitler and the Nazis wanted to murder all Jews *because* they were Jews. Not because of their faith, not despite their faith. But because of what Hitler called their "race." He did not believe this "inferior" people had any right to share the earth with their "superiors," the Germans. So Jews—religious and unreligious—were exterminated. They were killed even when their deaths proved harmful, militarily or economically, to the Nazis. It was a crime against all humanity, committed upon the body of the Jewish people. That the Jews were the victim this time derives from the long history of anti-Semitism.

How could it have happened?

It did not occur in a vacuum. It was the logical outcome of certain conditions of life. Given the antihuman nature of Nazi beliefs, the crime of the Holocaust could be expected. We see that now. That it happened once, unbelievable as it seems, means it could happen again. Hitler made it a possibility for anyone. Neither the Jews nor any other group on earth can feel safe from that crime in the future.

I do not believe that the world of Hitler was totally alien to the world we know. Still, before we can compare Hitler's Germany to anything else, we need to find out what it was like and how it came to be. And just as important, we need to expand our knowledge of our own human nature to understand why people were infected by Nazism, how the poison spread, and what its effects were. The question has to do with good and evil, with our inner being, with our power to make moral choices.

No one of us can know the whole truth. It is not made up merely of facts and figures. We have an abundance of that kind of evidence now, for the hell of Nazi Europe has become one of the most fully documented crimes in history. One can read the cold record for endless hours. The better path to the truth is through the eyewitness accounts—the letters, diaries, journals, and memoirs of those who experienced the terror and grief. This book will rely upon them. However inadequate words are, human language is all we have to reach across barriers to understanding.

BOOK ONE

History of Hatred

1

Not Citizens, Only Subjects

Jude verrecke . . . Jew perish . . .

How did it come to that? And why in Germany?

Germany is the country where modern anti-Semitism of the racist kind began. The term itself, "anti-Semitism," was first used only a few years before Hitler was born. But the roots of anti-Semitism go much farther back in history. The religious basis for it in the Christian world is the accusation (it appears in the Gospels) that the Jews were to blame for the crucifixion of Jesus. "Christ-killer" became a synonym for Jew. The anti-Semites took that charge as sanction for the persecution of the Jews.

In the early fourth century, Constantine the Great made Christianity the state religion of the Byzantine Empire. The Church insisted that Christianity was the true religion, the only religion, and demanded the conversion of the Jews. When the Jews would not easily give up their faith, the Church used the power of the State to make them outcasts. They were denied citizenship and its rights. By the end of the century, Jews were viewed as devils, cursed by God.

A popular and enduring hatred of the Jews built up. If Jews suffered misfortune, it was only divine punishment for Christ's crucifixion. But the punishment was not left to God alone. Both Church and State took legislative steps—later imitated in Hitler's edicts—to ensure Jewish misery. Among them were decrees that made it impossible for Jews to farm the land or to engage in the

3

crafts. Trade was almost the only choice left, and many Jews became merchants, working with and through other Jews scattered throughout the world.

As the economy of the medieval world developed, the Church lifted the restrictions it had placed on commercial activity, and Christians replaced Jews. The Church still forbade Christians to receive interest on loans, so the Jews provided the service of banking. But when banking profits became attractive, the Church eased its restrictions, and Christians then competed with Jews in finance, too. Yet, even as Christians took over the same financial functions, they libeled the Jews as avaricious and heartless—the image perpetuated by Shakespeare's Shylock.

The launching of the Crusades in 1096 marked the beginning of an oppression that for duration and intensity would be unmatched until Hitler's time. The hordes of nobles, knights, monks, and peasants who set off to free the Holy Land from the Moslem infidels began their bloody work with "the infidels at home"—the Jews. Offering the choice of baptism or death, the Crusaders slaughtered Jews on a stunning scale. Those Jews who refused baptism and sacrificed themselves "to sanctify the Name of God" became martyrs who set an example of heroism for centuries to come. What had been done in the name of Christianity made very few in the Church feel regret when the fury ended. Nested in the popular mind was the conviction that such atrocities must have been deserved. Piety became a convenient excuse for plunder.

To make the Jew an ever easier target for mobs hunting down the "Christ-killer," the Church's Fourth Lateran Council in 1215 required Jews to wear a distinctive badge on their clothing. Now no Jews could escape humiliation. As public pariahs, they were blamed for everything that went wrong. "The guilty Jews"—the words were inseparable. Expulsion or extermination seemed to be the Jews' fate. What delayed their elimination was their usefulness. While their money could be diverted into the treasuries of king and noble, they were tolerated. When that value was gone, they were expelled. In England it happened in 1290, in France in 1306, in Spain in 1492.

It was in these centuries that Europe began moving from the medieval into the modern world. Epochal changes were taking place in economic, political, cultural, and religious life. But the mass of Jews remained cut off from the mainstream and isolated. They were compelled to live behind ghetto walls. A new humanism induced more tolerance, but not for the Jews. Persecution continued, followed often by expulsion.

The Jews of Spain and Portugal fled into Turkey, the Balkans, Palestine, northern Italy, and Holland. Some migrated to the New World, settling in Brazil and the West Indies, and soon in North America, too. The Jews of Germany made new homes in Eastern Europe. The Polish rulers welcomed them because they needed Jewish enterprise. Jews were allowed to become traders and financiers.

The flow east was heightened by the founding of Martin Luther's new faith in the sixteenth century. In his youth, Luther had been a champion of the Jews. When he failed to win them to Protestantism, he raged at them in a language that exceeded even Hitler's for violence. He renewed all the old charges—the Jews were poisoners, ritual murderers, usurers, parasites, devils. He called for the burning of their synagogues, the seizure of their books, and their expulsion from all of Germany. (Centuries later, Hitler would find it helpful to circulate Luther's anti-Jewish writings in mass editions.)

Even as Catholics warred with Protestants, a few brave souls dared to argue for toleration. The Dutch scholar Erasmus suggested that toleration among all Christians would mean a more humane faith. He could even conceive of being a friend to a Jew. New ideas about the rights of the common man emerged later, as the Industrial Revolution developed in Western Europe. A struggle for civil emancipation began. By then there were numbers of middle-class Jews eager to break free of the ghetto and to share in the civil rights promised by the movement for Enlightenment.

It was Germany's Jews who were the first to be touched by the Enlightenment. Frederick the Great, a despotic ruler and no lover of the Jews, realized that his Prussia could prosper by encouraging enterprising Jews to found new industries and build up commerce. Many Jews seized the opportunity offered and rose to prominence as manufacturers, merchants, and bankers. In dealing with Prussia's chief customer, France, the German Jews absorbed the ideas of the French Enlightenment and circulated them at home.

Young Jews, especially, responded to the promise of liberty, equality, and fraternity. But their elders feared that Christian Enlightenment would lead to the desertion of Judaism. Moses Mendelssohn sought to work out a compromise between loyalty to his Jewish faith and participation in the broader culture. A brilliant thinker, he had left the poverty of the Dessau ghetto at fourteen and gone to Berlin to master secular learning. While working as a bookkeeper in the silk business of a wealthy Jew, he won acclaim in Berlin society for his critical essays in philosophy. Soon he was Europe's most celebrated Jew. Through the printed word and the founding of Jewish schools combining religious and secular education, he and his disciples spread the Enlightenment to the Jews of Europe.

Inspired by his example, young Jews devoted themselves to modern education so that they could make a mark in Western culture. Cracks appeared in the ghetto walls even before the French Revolution of 1789, and Napoleon's armies finished the job, bearing the banners of freedom wherever they marched. They defeated the Prussians in 1806; and in 1812 Prussia issued the Edict of Emancipation, which made Jews citizens. Jews were to have all the rights of the dominant majority. But not for long. Napoleon's downfall brought powerful reaction in its wake. Emancipation was undone in many places. The ideals of the Enlightenment were drowned in a wave of German nationalism. To be a patriot now meant to be a product of German culture and a Christian. Again the Jew was defined as an outsider. He was viewed as a parasite feeding upon the German body, which could never absorb him. His political rights were cut down or taken away altogether. An endless stream of anti-Semitic books and pamphlets polluted the culture of Germany. Some of the most distinguished intellectuals contributed to it. Feeling against the

Jews mounted to the point of violence. The old cry, "Hep, hep, death to the Jews!" echoed again in Germany's streets.

Popular writing dropped all distinctions between the "good" Jew and the "bad" Jew. Even the baptized and assimilated Jew was not spared, for the anti-Semite now condemned all Jews. No longer was it a question of religion. It was the Jew's "race," his "blood," that damned him. A Jewish stereotype took shape in widely read novels. The Jew was depicted as puny and cowardly. The ugly features given the Jewish villain were said to be the outward sign of an evil soul.

The Germans built hatred of the Jews into what they considered to be an unchallengeable scientific system. A "theory" of anti-Semitism was created to lend scientific justification to their prejudice. Wilhelm Marr based his theory of anti-Semitism on racial identity. He said that Jews, or Semites, had an inborn character that made them a "slave race," while the Germans, or Aryans, were the "master race." The Jews couldn't help being morally and physically inferior because Nature had predetermined that. The lucky Aryans (he meant the Teutonic or Nordic peoples, such as the Germans, Austrians, Scandinavians, Dutch, English, and French) were by the same token born to be superior. The Aryans were the jewel of the world. Everything great and good was said to be the creation of this "master race."

Such nonsense, fed to the ignorant and unthinking, infuriated some scientists of that time. Max Müller, the noted German philologist and orientalist, said:

> It is but too easily forgotten that if we speak of Aryan and Semitic families, the ground of that classification is language and language only. There are Aryan and Semitic languages, but it is against all rules of logic to speak . . . of an Aryan race, of Aryan blood, or Aryan skulls, and to attempt ethnological classification on purely linguistic grounds.

The smashing victory over the French in the Franco-Prussian War in 1870 made many Germans feel they truly belonged to a "master race." And when Otto von Bismarck's policy of "blood and iron" succeeded in molding the petty states into the German Empire in 1871, it intensified that feeling of superiority. Chancellor Bismarck proclaimed the State's highest duty was to increase its own power. Germany's destiny was to conquer the world; "lesser" peoples had to be subdued.

Militarism and the doctrine of "blood and iron" became the dominant forces in German life. Under Bismarck's leadership, the educated classes turned away from rationalism and liberalism. A new kind of pseudo-scholarship, useful to politicians who prosper on myths, held sway. Two foreign writers, the Frenchman Arthur de Gobineau and the Englishman Houston Stewart Chamberlain, contributed props for the myth of racial superiority. De Gobineau held that the Jews were a "mongrel race." Chamberlain wrote that "The Jewish race is altogether bastardized, and its existence is a crime against the holy laws of life." Both men won vast audiences in Germany by singing the praises of the "Aryan race."

Politicians began to draw upon the power of anti-Semitism for their propaganda arsenal. In 1878 speakers for a Christian Social Workers' party fired up mass meetings by blaming Jews for business failures and profiteering. The party leader, Dr. Adolf Stöcker (court preacher to the Kaiser), coined the slogan *"Deutschland erwache!"*; Hitler would borrow it later. And as Hitler would, Stöcker directed his appeal to the lower middle classes—artisans, shopkeepers, clerks, petty officials—who yearned for better incomes and higher social status. In 1879 Wilhelm Marr founded the League of Anti-Semitism "to save the German fatherland from complete Judaization." A year later the anti-Semites were able to secure 300,000 signatures to a petition demanding that the government bar the Jews from all schools and universities and from holding public office.

By 1893 candidates of anti-Semitic political parties were able to muster 400,000 votes and elect many deputies to the Reichstag. A new slogan—"The Jews Are Our Misfortune"—appeared in print and on banners. Another philosopher, the anarchist Eugen Dühring, stepped forth to sound the final note in anti-Semitism. The Jews, he wrote, are "inferior and depraved. . . . The duty of the Nordic peoples is to exterminate such parasitic races as we exterminate snakes and beasts of prey."

His was a paranoid image of the Jew as the universal enemy. Entrenched as an article of German faith, it would have the destructive power of an atomic arsenal when Hitler triggered it.

2

Hitler's Magic Formula

Adolf Hitler was born in 1889 in an Austrian village across the border from German Bavaria. His father was a minor customs official who retired when Hitler was six and began moving about restlessly. The boy attended many schools in different towns. At eleven he was sent to a high school in Linz to study for the civil service. But he did not want to follow his father's course; he desired to become an artist. His grades fell off and he dropped out. His father died in 1903, leaving his widow Klara a tiny pension on which to support Adolf and his sister.

Adolf would not find a job to help his mother out. For three years he roved the countryside. By sixteen, he showed an interest in politics as well as a hatred for all the non-German subject peoples who lived within the Austro-Hungarian Empire. In 1907 he was rejected by an art school in Vienna because he showed no promise. That same year his mother died.

Homeless and penniless, Hitler spent four despairing years in Vienna. He lived in flophouses and ate in charity kitchens. Vienna was thriving then, and he could have earned a living if he had wished. Instead, he gave all his time to voracious reading, mostly German history and mythology. The ideas of Fichte, Hegel, de Gobineau, and Houston Stewart Chamberlain, soaked up in his youth, became the stuff of his later writings and speeches. But how this young man became the demonic figure whose incredible willpower and hypnotic influence led to the greatest crimes in history has never been explained. The circumstances of his childhood and youth—are these enough to account for it? Why Hitler, then, and not the many others whose early lives paralleled his?

In 1913, Hitler left Vienna for Germany. He wanted to escape military service in the Austrian army because he refused to bear arms with Jews, Czechs, and Slavs. The longer he lived in Vienna, he wrote, "the more my hatred grew for the foreign mixture of peoples which had begun to corrode the old site of German culture."

At the age of twenty-four, he came to Munich. A year later the First World War exploded, and Hitler wrote that "[I] sank down on my knees, thanked heaven out of the fullness of my heart for giving me the good fortune to be permitted to live in such a time." Now he could shoulder arms for his adopted Fatherland in a war that would destroy untold millions.

The huge German armies swept through Belgium and northern France, but the swift total conquest planned by the German General Staff did not occur. The two-front war—against Russia in the east and France, Britain, and finally the United States in the west—bogged down in seas of mud and blood. As German victory failed to come, the tensions the Bismarck system had suppressed boiled up to the surface. The German economy was in ruins and people faced starvation. Political leaders asked why the masses should make all the sacrifices for an autocratic regime. The Emperor made promises of reform, but they came too late. The radical parties were calling not only for an end to the war but for a democratic socialist republic. The German fleet mutinied, and troops on the western front refused to fight anymore. Antiwar strikes and demonstrations broke out all over Germany. With defeat in the field and support melting away at home, the General Staff entered negotiations with the Allies and accepted their peace terms. Kaiser Wilhelm II abdicated and fled to Holland. Bismarck's German Empire was in ruins.

To Corporal Hitler, who had fought in many battles throughout the long war and earned the Iron Cross for bravery, the news of final defeat was a shocking blow. He, like countless other

Germans fed on the myth of German invincibility, could not believe his beloved army had lost. Germany's defeat must have been caused by betrayal at home. The liberals, the democrats, the radicals, the Jews—they were to blame for this incredible calamity.

The Treaty of Versailles reflected the fact of German defeat. Its terms included the return of territories seized by Germany from others, the reduction of the army and navy to small forces, the outlawing of the General Staff, and payment for war costs and damages. In signing, Germany was forced to admit it had been the aggressor in this war.

All the German parties joined in bitterly denouncing the Versailles treaty, forgetting it was not as harsh as the Treaty of Brest Litovsk, which the Germans had imposed on the Russians in this same war. Unfortunately, instead of placing the responsibility for disaster where it belonged, on the General Staff and the Empire's rulers, the German people turned against the new republic struggling to rise from the ashes of defeat. The legend grew that the German army had not lost on the battlefield but had been "stabbed in the back" by evil forces behind the lines—speculators, radicals, politicians, and Jews.

The democratic constitution which Germany adopted in 1919 at the old cultural center of Weimar was one of the most advanced in political history. But it was only a piece of paper. The social cement needed to make it effective was missing. Germany was a fiercely divided society, torn between extremes of radical and right-wing thought and separated by rigid class, regional, and religious lines. Whoever governed Germany would have to meet mountainous problems.

The Weimar Constitution turned out to have many weaknesses. Its democratic provisions were almost destroyed by Article 48. This allowed the President to scrap the entire bill of rights in emergencies and to rule by decree. Thus, upon the whim of whoever held the office, the Constitution could be invalidated and dictatorship take over.

The Weimar Republic, as it was called, staggered from the beginning under the humiliating weight of defeat and the Versailles treaty. The German people were badly prepared for any form of democracy. Even as great an artist as the novelist Thomas Mann could write in 1918, "Away with the foreign and repulsive slogan 'democratic.' The mechanical democratic political institutions of the West will never take root here."

In the four years immediately following the war, Germany's economy was shattered, and the middle class almost destroyed. As unemployment and misery spread, the German people listened to voices that promised a quick end to their troubles. Radical sections of the working class wanted to follow the example of Russia, where the Communist, or Bolshevik, party had seized power and set up a dictatorship. But the German Socialists followed a moderate policy, and from them came the republic's most solid support. Still, many Germans held the Weimar Republic in contempt because it was not curing economic ills and because it had not restored Germany to the status of a great power.

Politics was ridiculed as a hypocritical and dirty business good people must shun. So the vital decisions were left to governmental authorities. Politics degenerated into brutal and bloody street battles for power. There were hundreds of political assassinations in those years, few of the guilty punished. Extremists of the right wing got away with literal murder, while liberals were sentenced to long prison terms on trumped-up charges of "treason."

After the war Hitler found a job with a Munich regiment, propagandizing the soldiers against democracy and socialism. He also served the army by informing on "subversive" groups. That was how he encountered the German Workers' party (suspected of being subversive because of that word "worker") at a meeting in a beer cellar. Seeing that the tiny group shared his ideas about racism and anti-Semitism and espoused his militant nationalism, he joined its executive committee.

At once Hitler showed his enormous talent as an orator. It is hard to understand his effectiveness when one listens today to recordings of his radio speeches. His voice is shrill, hysterical, coarse. His speeches seem only a string of slogans. And his physical appearance was unimpressive, too. Pictures show him as short and flabby, and that little toothbrush mustache is ridiculous. Many who knew him have said that his mind was mediocre. He liked nothing better than to eat sweets and talk about his loyal dogs and his war record. Movie musicals were his favorite entertainment.

Whatever it was, something about Hitler persuaded people, even in these early 1920s, to regard him as their messiah. His magnetism became one of his greatest weapons in building a political party that would carry him to power. He soon renamed it the National Socialist German Workers' party, or Nazi party. He organized strong-arm squads to guard his own meetings from hecklers and to break up rival meetings. These squads, known as the SA, or Storm Troopers, were built up over the years into a huge private army. Hitler chose the party symbol, the swastika. This ancient hooked cross was emblazoned on Nazi uniforms, arm bands, posters, flags, and banners. Eventually it decorated even dog collars, bed sheets, matchbooks, and water glasses.

Within two years Hitler was sole master of the Nazi party, the leader whose wish and word were absolute law to his followers. Party membership grew slowly at first. Funds came from collections and meetings and from party dues—probably, too, from secret army contributions. Soon the movement had its own newspaper, the *People's Guardian*, to spread its propaganda more widely.

When inflation made German currency worthless in 1923, the buying power of wages and salaries was reduced to nothing. The hungry, desperate Germans blamed the government and democracy itself for the disaster. Amid the chaos, Hitler saw his chance to make a bid for power. With General Ludendorff, he engineered the "beer-hall putsch" in Munich in November 1923. This attempt to overthrow the government was quickly stopped by the German army. The Nazi party was suppressed, and Hitler was tried for treason. During his three-week trial he spoke out boldly and made himself a national figure through the press. He declared he was only trying to crush the Communists and Socialists—the Marxism that had caused the ruin of Germany. "I feel myself not a traitor," he told the court, "but a German who wished the best for his people." He was treated lightly, and served only nine months in a comfortable cell.

In prison Hitler wrote much of his book, Mein Kampf (My Struggle). It told the story of his early struggles and outlined what he meant to do to create a new Germany. He did not conceal his aims. He wanted to reunite Germany and Austria on the racial principle that "people of the same blood should be in the same Reich." If the reunited people should lack Lebensraum (living space), "then can the moral right arise, from the need of the people, to acquire foreign territory. The plough is then the sword; and the tears of war will produce the daily bread for generations to come."

To carry out his life's work, he said, "every possible means should be employed." He meant just that: every possible means.

In his book Hitler speaks of the Jews as parasites on the bodies of other peoples, conspiring to achieve a world dictatorship. Through financial manipulation the Jews were gaining economic control of Germany; through Marxism they were controlling the socialist parties and the trade unions. The Nazis, said Hitler, aimed to eradicate this alien race.

In the program Hitler's party had announced in 1920, 7 of the 25 points dealt with the Jews. The program called for the denial of citizenship and public office to Jews, the expulsion of Jews who had immigrated, and the exclusion of Jews from the press. All German Jews were categorized as "foreigners" and "guests" of the nation.

Hitler used anti-Semitism brilliantly, if insanely, to reconcile all contradictions and oppositions. It was the force which cemented together such disparate elements as workers and industrialists, land barons and peasants, fools and intellectuals, socialists and capitalists, radicals and conservatives, atheists and preachers, young and old. It was a magic formula to solve all social problems. It was a weapon against all opposition. Anyone who differed with Hitler was a Jew or a stooge of the Jews.

The Catholic historian of anti-Semitism, Father Edward H. Flannery, points out how this brand of anti-Semitism differed from earlier forms:

Hitlerian or Nazi anti-Semitism was something beyond the older kind. . . . This radical and nihilistic Jew-hatred preached with a boundless fury and coarseness was essentially new. No longer was the Jew a mere scapegoat or member of an inferior race, but the cause of every problem, the destroyer, the poisoner of Aryan blood, the epitome of evil. And he was all this inherently and uneradicably; neither baptism nor renunciation of Judaism could redeem him. The solution to the Jewish problem was also new and simple, and concisely summarized in the Nazi slogan, "Jude verrecke!"

But did it really differ? Or was it only the last step in a progression that had begun with the early Christian saints? Raul Hilberg, an historian of the Holocaust, has outlined the steps:

The missionaries of Christianity had said in effect: You have no right to live among us as Jews. The secular rulers who followed had proclaimed: You have no right to live among us. The German Nazis at last decreed: You have no right to live.

Hitler had learned a great lesson from the failure of the Munich uprising in 1923. No longer would he call for an open physical attack on the citadel of power. Mounting the barricades was romantic foolishness in the age of the machine gun. It was suicidal to smash head-on into the army and the rulers of the state. He would use trickery instead. "Democracy," he said, "must be defeated with the weapons of democracy." He would have his revolution, but *after*, not before, he came to power.

Hitler had no new or original ideas. Neither in *Mein Kampf* nor in the Nazi party program is there any coherent ideology. He mouthed what all the other reactionary politicians were saying. His call for *Lebensraum* and for the expulsion of the Jews was the common stock-in-trade of all the right-wing parties. Several recent studies of Nazi history conclude that Hitler had no blueprint for a totalitarian state. He improvised hastily to meet each crisis, both in his rise to power and in his exercise of that power once he attained it.

While never letting up on his rabid anti-Semitism, Hitler offered something for everybody except, of course, the Jews. To workers he promised jobs; to employers, fatter profits and freedom from union restraints; to the lower middle class, status and self-respect; to the generals, a glorious army; to Germany, world supremacy; to the nations abroad, peace. He was the master demagogue; he understood crowd psychology; he knew how to manipulate issues, to mobilize the disaffected. The mass of his followers came from the poor, the youth, the small tradesmen, and the handicraftsmen.

Promising everything to everybody means promising nothing to anybody. But in the hot pursuit of power, it did not matter. Hitler himself, not the program, was the sole unifying force. Despair with things as they were united his followers with their mystical leader. No one stopped to discuss what would be done once power was attained.

In the last half of the 1920s, the German economy had a striking recovery, financed largely by foreign funds. German industry was rebuilt. The government followed the traditional policy of paternalism in industry, housing, agriculture, and labor. These more normal times were lean years for the Nazis. Hitler seemed unimportant and his party was powerless. Still, the membership hung on, growing slowly, and the lieutenants Hitler needed stayed with him.

Then the worldwide depression that began in 1929 hit Germany with devastating force. Again the people were plunged into despair. In the Reichstag election of 1930, the Nazi vote shot up from about a million to over six million; the number of Nazi deputies, from 12 to 107. The Nazis were no longer a fringe party but the second largest party. This was a clear sign that the German people hungered for new leadership.

But why did they turn to Hitler? Why to the Nazis and not the other right-wing nationalist parties who advocated much the same program? One answer seems to be Hitler's greater credibility. The German masses believed he, and not the others, could deliver what he promised. They recognized him as one of them. He too had been a common soldier; he too had known life's failures. He talked their language, and he spoke with passionate conviction. He made them believe that his will, and his will alone, could solve all their problems and save Germany.

Marching along the streets to take their seats in the Reichstag, the new Nazi deputies threw rocks into Jewish store windows. In the parliamentary chamber they chanted, "Germany awake! Jew perish!" A fourth of the population had not enough to eat. Millions were on relief. Hitler seemed, to many, a Siegfried returned to earth to avenge the defeat of 1918 and lead the Germans to prosperity. He renewed his savage propaganda against the paralyzed government. "Democracy," he sneered, "is a rule by crazy brains. The German Republic is a monstrosity."

By 1932 there were 6 million jobless in Germany. The deepening crisis pushed the Nazi party ahead. That year its vote went up to nearly 14 million, and 230 Nazi Brownshirts were seated in the Reichstag. The Nazis were now the largest party in Germany but still unable to win a·clear majority. They stood on the threshold of power. The right-wing clique around the senile President Hindenburg (in his mid-eighties now) speculated that Hitler's mass support might be the means of shoring up the crumbling government. Hitler sat down for talks with them.

He might have been stopped even now if the other German parties—the Social Democrats, the Communists, the Nationalists, the Catholic Center—had united against him. After all, he had never won more than 37 percent of the popular vote. But the other parties' leaders failed to see that their political differences were nothing compared to the terrible menace of Nazism. When the other leaders remained hopelessly divided, Hitler was able to make the political bargains that won him the post of Chancellor.

On January 30, 1933, Nazism had its miracle. Scarcely a dozen years before, with a handful of other unknown men, Hitler had founded the Nazi party. Now, on this historic night, in the flickering light of thousands of torches, endless columns of Brownshirts, flanked by cheering crowds, paraded through the streets of Berlin.

At the chancellery window stood the delighted Hitler, arm outstretched in the Nazi salute. "No power on earth," he vowed that night, "shall bring me out of here alive."

Ein Volk,
Ein Reich, Ein Führer!

Hitler's first aim in office was to consolidate his power. He moved at once to fulfill the Nazi slogan: *EIN VOLK, EIN REICH, EIN FÜHRER!** (*ONE PEOPLE, ONE GOVERNMENT, ONE LEADER!*) First, he imposed a universal ban on demonstrations. His right-hand man, Hermann Goering, took control of the regular police and the Nazi secret police, the Gestapo. Goering, a fighter pilot in World War I, was a beefy blusterer with great energy who helped Hitler capture power. "My measures will not be hindered by any legal considerations or bureaucracy whatsoever," he said. "It is not justice that I have to carry out but annihilation and extermination."

In February 1933 the Reichstag building was set on fire by secret order of Joseph Goebbels, Hitler's propaganda chief. The crime was called a Communist plot. The next day, Hitler persuaded President Hindenburg to sign an "emergency" decree empowering the government to suspend all civil rights. Now Hitler could arrest and even execute any suspicious person. Thousands of Communists, Socialists, liberals, and trade unionists were dragged off to jails or to abandoned warehouses and factory basements. Many of them were beaten or tortured to death. The non-Nazi press was banned. Under these conditions of hysteria and fear, a national election was held on March 5. The Nazis got 17

* *Führer* is the German spelling. Except in German quotations, the English spelling *Fuehrer* is used throughout this book.

million votes, still not a clear majority. Nevertheless, by throwing the elected Communist deputies out of their seats and joining with the Nationalists and the Catholic Center, the Nazis succeeded in obtaining the two-thirds majority vote in the Reichstag needed to make Hitler legal dictator. (It was the last meaningful act of the German parliament. From then on it was nothing but a cheering section for Hitler's speeches.) Next, Hitler abolished every political party but his own; he dissolved the trade unions, seized their funds and headquarters, and jailed their leaders. Labor in Germany became slavery in all but name. With the abolition of the unions went the right to strike, to collective bargaining, even to shift jobs. The National Labor Front made all the decisions. Wages sank while profits rose. Despite their Socialist or Communist tradition, the workers accepted the brutal discipline, perhaps because Hitler had wiped out unemployment through his vast public works and rearmament programs and by drafting youth into the armed forces.

Having reduced German labor to serfdom, Hitler turned to capital. All the financial institutions were taken over by the state, and industry was mobilized for rearmament. Total control of newspapers, magazines, books, radio, and film was given to the Ministry of Propaganda and Popular Enlightenment, headed by Joseph Goebbels.

Goebbels was a tiny figure, scarcely five feet tall and weighing under a hundred pounds, with a bad limp from childhood polio. He had a degree from the University of Heidelberg and aspired to become one of Germany's literary greats. But his true talent lay in creating not art but propaganda. He understood the power of propaganda. It had nothing to do with truth, he said. "The propaganda which produces the desired results is good and all other propaganda is bad. Therefore, it is beside the point to say your propaganda is too crude, too mean, too brutal, or too unfair, for all this does not matter. . . . Propaganda is always a means to an end."

As Hitler's chief "enlightener," Goebbels banned all democratic literature. On May 10, 1933, gangs of Nazi youths ripped out of the libraries the works of all authors on Goebbels' blacklist. By the truckload, they took what was best in German and non-German literature to the Berlin square where the opera house faced the university, and set the books on fire as thousands of students cheered. One among those whose books they burned—the poet Heinrich Heine—once wrote, "When they burn books, in the end it is man that they burn."

The only obstacle still in Hitler's way was the left wing of his own party, headed by Ernst Roehm. Roehm wanted a "Second Revolution" to take over big business and the landed estates. Had not Hitler made such radical promises in his climb to power? But now the Fuehrer wanted to use those forces, not alienate them. Fearing that the SA, headed by Roehm and over 2-million strong, might get out of control, Hitler arranged for the Gestapo to murder Roehm. Added to the death list were many other political, as well as personal, enemies. Over 1,000 men and women fell victim to the blood purge that took place on June 30, 1934.

When President Hindenburg died in August, Hitler was able to toss away the last scrap of constitutionalism. He immediately united the offices of President and Chancellor and proclaimed himself Supreme Head of State and Commander-in-Chief of the Armed Forces. He demanded and received from the army and all servants of the state a "sacred oath" of "unconditional obedience." Then he asked the German people to approve by plebiscite; 90 percent voted "Yes." He was master now. Germany was under the personal rule of one man, Adolf Hitler. Every time Germans exchanged the greeting—"Heil Hitler!"—it was a recognition of that fact. His supremacy was felt in every sphere of political and personal life.

Although the Nazi apparatus had swelled enormously, the Party alone was not enough to carry out Hitler's goals. Nazis penetrated the most crucial organizations, making deals or concessions to gain full cooperation. The big institutions were let alone, as long as they followed governmental policy. Hitler preferred not to disturb the army, industry, or the civil service. Kept intact, they could be made to carry out his aims.

Alongside these existing institutions was the Party's political and social machinery. Its leaders built up their own personal empires until there were at least four major power complexes: economic development, centering on Goering; labor, on Robert Ley; the police, on Heinrich Himmler; and propaganda, on Goebbels. The four men acted with considerable independence, because Hitler hated the details of administration. Complicated by personal rivalries and jealousies, the system nevertheless worked with astonishing success. In just six years the productive and military power of Germany was developed to the point where Hitler was ready to challenge the world.

Party membership, a million when Hitler began his rule, was carefully regulated. The only basic Party rules, said Hitler, were "blind discipline and the absolute recognition of authority." Goering expressed what that meant: "I have no personal conscience; Adolf Hitler is my only conscience." At its peak the Party included nearly 7 million members. For most positions of authority in Germany, Nazi party membership was essential. Expulsion was therefore a serious matter. The Party was organized by region and reached down into the neighborhood. Every block had its Nazi agent to spy on the people's thoughts and behavior. Everyone in Germany—child, youth, or adult—was touched somehow by the vast Party network.

The Nazis sought to mold the young, from infancy, into a race of "true" Germans. "It is my duty," Hitler said, "to make use of every means of training the German people to cruelty, and to prepare them for war. . . . A violently active, dominating, intrepid, brutal youth—that is what I am after. Youth must be all this. It must be indifferent to pain. There must be no weakness or tenderness in it." There were separate organizations for very young boys and girls; and at fourteen, the boys joined the Hitler Youth. An exciting life of marching, singing, saluting, camping, physical training, and sports captured youths' loyalty early. At eighteen, the young men began six months' compulsory-labor service in a camp (women also did labor service), followed by two years of military service.

Children quickly responded to the poisonous Nazi propaganda. Bella Fromm was a prominent Berlin journalist with many friends in high places. Perhaps that was why, although Jewish, she was still allowed to work. One evening she was having dinner with old non-Jewish friends. At the table were Ilse and Otto Kapp, and Ilse's brother, with his two daughters. The young girls were fond of "Aunt Bella." These passages from the Fromm diary for October 1935 are a token of the vicious spying and informing that had become common in Germany:

Inge and Lolo, the two little girls, sat at table with us. Inge had not come to see me for weeks. I asked her why, though I had a feeling that I knew the answer.

Inge looked at me as though trying to visualize me all over again. "Aunt Bella," she said, "you don't really seem so—so fiendish."

Her father reprimanded her with a stern glance. "Don't blame the child," I interceded for her. "I know what they teach her in school."

Relieved, the little one chatted on without inhibition. "I told Herr Runge, that's our teacher, that you weren't like that, Aunt Bella. So he said we didn't understand how wicked you really were. Then for the rest of the lesson, he read to us out of a book about Jews . . . that they are evil . . . they look like devils . . . they should all be killed. He said we should spit at them whenever we see them."

Blond, delicate, sweet Inge! The words, though not her own, came strangely from her lips.

"On our way home," Inge continued, "Ursel and I saw an old woman. She looked very poor, and we thought she might be Jewish. Ursel said we should spit at her. So we ran up to her and Ursel spat on her coat. . . . it was an old coat . . . torn. . . . I didn't spit, Aunt Bella. I thought it was disgusting. Ursel yelled at her: 'Old Jew witch!' She says that tomorrow she will tell the teacher I wouldn't spit, too."

We sat there in silence for a moment or two. Then I said: "Inge, darling, you are intelligent enough to know that evil has nothing to do with the race a person is born into. It is God who decides whether you are to be a Jew or a Christian. There are nasty people everywhere, but most people are the same,

whether they are Catholic, Protestant, or Jewish. All worship
the same God . . . the God of Love."

"I won't do it," said Inge quietly. "I won't do it. Even if they
punish me."

"That's right," said her father. "I wouldn't want you to. If
you could do it, I would never want to see you again."

Five days later, Ilse Kapp, pale and disturbed, came to see Bella
Fromm:

"I did not come before everything was settled. The day after
our talk with Inge, Herr Runge [the teacher] discussed the
Jewish question again. 'Inge,' he said, 'do you admit that all
Jews are damnable and vile?'

" 'No,' insisted Inge.

"Herr Runge became increasingly aggressive. Inge ever more
frightened. 'Daddy says I am right,' she said.

"That same night the Gestapo came to take my brother away.
We did everything in our power. He escaped with a severe
warning, and some horrible scars on his body. I have just been
to his house to see him."

It was not only children who responded to Nazi propaganda.
Each September at Nuremberg, the week-long Party rally demon-
strated "the most frenzied adulation for a public figure" the
American reporter William L. Shirer said he had ever seen.
Watching it in 1934, Shirer observed:

Like a Roman emperor Hitler rode into this medieval town
at sundown today past solid phalanxes of wildly cheering
Nazis. . . . Tens of thousands of Swastika flags blot out the
Gothic beauty of the place. . . . The streets are a sea of brown
and black uniforms. . . . I got caught in a mob of ten thousand
hysterics who jammed the moat in front of Hitler's hotel,
shouting: "We want our Fuehrer!" I was a little shocked at
the faces, especially those of the women, when Hitler finally
appeared on the balcony for a moment. . . . They looked up

at him as if he was a Messiah, their faces transformed into something positively inhuman. . . . He is restoring pageantry, color and mysticism to the drab lives of the twentieth century Germans. . . .

Shirer attended the mass rally in a great hall:

Hitler's arrival was dramatic. The band stopped playing. There was a hush over the thirty thousand people packed in the hall. Then the band struck up the "Badenweiler March," a very catchy tune and used only when Hitler makes his big entries. Hitler appeared in the back of the auditorium, and followed by his aides, Goering, Goebbels, Hess, Himmler, and the others, he strode slowly down the long center aisle while thirty thousand hands were raised in salute. . . . Then an immense symphony orchestra played Beethoven's Egmont Overture. Great Klieg lights played on the stage, where Hitler sat surrounded by a hundred party officials and officers of the army and navy. Behind them the "blood flag," the one carried down the streets of Munich in the ill-fated putsch. Behind this, four or five hundred SA standards. When the music was over, Rudolf Hess, Hitler's closest confidant, rose and slowly read the names of the Nazi "martyrs"—Brownshirts who had been killed in the struggle for power—a rollcall of the dead, and the thirty thousand seemed very moved.

In such an atmosphere no wonder, then, that every word dropped by Hitler seemed like an inspired Word from on high . . . and every lie pronounced is accepted as high truth itself.

Later in the rally an immense chanting chorus of 50,000 youths from the Labor Corps, shiny spades on their shoulders, broke into a perfect goose-step and with one voice intoned, WE WANT ONE LEADER! NOTHING FOR US! EVERYTHING FOR GERMANY! HEIL HITLER!

Women were relegated by Hitler to the function of breeding machines. Their duty was to present the Fatherland with as many soldiers as possible. Under Nazism, antifeminism was a kind of secondary racism. Women were considered naturally inferior, like non-Germans and non-Aryans. Motherhood was the prime patriotic, as well as moral, virtue. When women were not busy in that role, then they must do the work women were "naturally" inclined to: farm labor, domestic service, sales help. The one place, especially, women did not belong was in politics. From the beginning, women were kept out of leadership in the Party. But even within the Party's *Frauenschaft* (Women's Organization), a feminist countermovement surfaced which dared to criticize male domination. Such voices were soon silenced.

To gain control of the army, Hitler Nazified it at the top, putting in generals devoted to his regime. He drew both the civil service and business more directly under Party and state influence. The machinery of power carried on the routine of government while it advanced the aims of Nazism. But Hitler also had at his command a huge apparatus for coercion—secret police, imprisonment, concentration camps, execution. The chief instruments for coercion penetrated every corner of German life. Nazi agents spied on everyday behavior, policed the performance of Party and state tasks, ran concentration camps, and later carried out mass killings. To squirm out of the reach of this vast network, this police state, was almost impossible.

The Gestapo (*Geheime Staatspolizei*), organized by Goering, was not concerned with ordinary crime. Its mission was to suppress independent thought and to eliminate all opposition.

The SS (*Schutzstaffel*) was the Blackshirted security service led by Himmler. It started out in the 1920s as a special guard for Hitler, and developed into an elite of Nazi fanatics. Its men were recruited from the aristocracy, the intelligentsia, and the middle class. Chosen for physique and devotion to the Fuehrer's goals, members of the SS were trained to consider themselves the "super race." The SS had its own courts, its own press, and finally its own military branch, the *Waffen-SS*. It built a reputation as the most merciless instrument of terror. By 1936 Himmler's fanatical efficiency won him supreme command not only of the SS but of the Gestapo and the criminal police.

Himmler, the son of a Bavarian schoolmaster, was brought up as a devout Catholic. He served in the army briefly at the end of World War I, then bought a small chicken farm and became a fertilizer salesman. He was a veteran of the Munich putsch and the most dogged disciple of Hitler's racism. He turned easily from breeding chickens to planning the breeding of a "master race." Short, pudgy, stupid-faced, he did not resemble his ideal Aryan. He was an ignorant and bloodless man, indifferent to cruelty. When he heard objections to what went on in his torture chambers, he would say that his victims were only "animals" or "criminals." He was the type of man ready to sacrifice humanity for an abstract ideal. The horrors done in the name of safeguarding the "master race" never disturbed his complacency.

As boss of all the security forces, Himmler also held the strings of the third major instrument of terror, the SD (*Sicherheitsdienst*). It was designed as a security service for the SS and kept small. Its 3,000 operatives controlled 100,000 informers, who spied on the private lives of the German people, including Party members.

The SD's chief was Reinhard Heydrich. A blond giant of a man, he took Himmler's fancy as the ideal Aryan. In 1932, at the age of twenty-eight, Heydrich began organizing his intelligence network. Brilliant and coldhearted, he had a keen eye for the ambitions and weaknesses of the Nazi leadership. He played them against one another to his own advantage.

Concentration camps were created in the earliest days of the Hitler regime as places to hold people in "protective custody." A decree allowed the Gestapo to send anyone to a concentration camp for as long a time as the Gestapo pleased, without trial or conviction, even if a court had already absolved the person of guilt or if the person had already served his sentence in prison. The law—a joke to call it that!—let the Gestapo do with people whatever it wished. This meant mass control by terror. The true function of the concentration camps was to eliminate every form of active or potential opposition.

By the end of 1933, there were at least 50 camps spread throughout Germany. These early camps were the forerunners of the later labor camps and the death camps. In the beginning, many victims were given a bad beating and then ransomed to family or friends. It was intimidation combined with blackmail. Sometimes the prisoners were murdered, because they were considered too dangerous, or out of sheer sadism. At first the camps were controlled by the Gestapo.

By mid-1934, however, Hitler gave the SS control of the camps. As leaders of the "master race," the SS had no qualms about treating camp inmates any way they liked. The terror began with segregation and humiliation and went on to torture and murder. They beat, flayed, strangled, shot, and gassed their victims. Their goal was to exterminate enemies. Any means would serve the purpose. At first, some Germans thought the camps would disappear when opposition faded, especially after the Roehm purge. But instead, their number grew steadily. By 1936, camps were being planned for permanence. The designers worked out camp quarters for the prisoners, barracks for the guards, and housing projects for the SS officers, all as a unit. In the years before World War II, the camps whose names conjured up the greatest fear were Dachau near Munich, Buchenwald near Weimar, Sachsenhausen near Berlin, and Ravensbruck near Mecklenburg.

The camps held three types of prisoners. The "politicals" were the Communists, Social Democrats, Jehovah's Witnesses, opposition clergymen, people who talked against the regime, and purged Nazis. The second group were the "asocials," primarily habitual criminals and sex offenders. The last group were members of "inferior races," the Jews and the Gypsies. Children too, by the tens of thousands, were imprisoned in the concentration camps, with or without their parents. About 15 percent were under the age of twelve; the others were between twelve and eighteen.

The Nazis did not arrest all German Jews during this period. Sometimes there were mass roundups which put many Jews into camps. Or individual Jews were picked up because they were "politicals" or fitted into some other category. But in whatever camp they were placed, the Jews stayed in segregated barracks and were given the most menial tasks.

All prisoners wore prescribed markings on their clothes to indicate their category. These were a serial number and colored triangles, both sewn on the left shirt breast and the right trouser leg. The triangles pointed down. Red denoted politicals; green, criminals; purple, Jehovah's Witnesses; black, "shiftless elements"; pink, homosexuals. The classification triangle for Jews was yellow. It had to be sewn on point-up, so that if a Jew were placed in another category as well, the two triangles would form a six-pointed Star of David. Non-Jews of various categories were mixed together within the individual camps, on the principle of divide-and-rule.

The Nazis used a deliberately senseless system in the camps to rob prisoners of their dignity and humanity. Emil Fackenheim, twenty-two, was one of those sent to the Sachsenhausen camp. The prisoners worked daily in a tile factory outside the camp. The work seemed like ordinary labor directed to a purpose. But then, he says:

> . . . Many a day we spent carrying sand—always on the double!
> —from place A to place B, only in order to be ordered the next
> day to carry it back from place B to place A. The senselessness
> of this labor was so obvious that everyone understood it. . . .
> We kept our morale through humor. We knew that this system
> had no purpose. Hence we also knew that its only purpose
> could be torture for torture's sake—to break us down. And
> aware of this purpose, we resisted it.
>
> I recall an incident early in our imprisonment (when we
> were still quite naive) when a well-known Berlin rabbi and I
> lined up outside the medical barrack for treatment for a sore
> or infected leg (I forget which). After a while the Nazi medical
> officer came out, kicked us with his jackboots and shouted,
> "Run, Jews!" As we were running, the rabbi turned to me and
> asked, "Are you still sick?"

Another inmate of Sachsenhausen, sent there at the same time, was Dr. K. J. Ball-Kaduri. A favorite amusement of the Nazi guards, he recalls, was to stand him up and force him to bellow again and again this "poem":

Dear old Moses, come again,
Lead your Jewish fellowmen
Once more to their promised land.
Split once more for them the sea,
Two huge columns let it be
Fixed as firmly as two walls.
When the Jews are all inside
On their pathway, long and wide,
Shut the trap, Lord, do your best!
Give us the world its lasting rest!

Fackenheim notes that this "poem" was not the creation of Nazi anti-Semitism, but something handed down from the 1880s, from Dr. Adolf Stöcker's Christian anti-Semitism. "It was simply humanly impossible," he says, "first for German Jews, then for European Jews, to recognize that the enemies were so many and so vicious. Hence, on the Jewish side, wishful thinking, and on the Nazi side, its systematic exploitation."

4

"The Protection of German Blood and German Honor"

With his hand on the lever of power, Hitler began a progressive terror against the Jews.

How many Jews did Germany contain? In 1933, there were half a million—less than 1 percent of the population. But ignoring how few they were, the Nazis had charged day in and day out that the Jews dominated industry, finance, and government.

Did they? Not one of the most powerful German industries—Krupp, Klöckner, Siemens, Stinnes, I. G. Farben, Hugenberg, Vereinigte Stahlwerke, Hapag, Stumm, Nordlloyd—was in Jewish hands. And the international cartels which German industries were part of—oil, iron, potash, chemicals, shipping—Jews had no influence in them, either as owners or directors. Tick off the most powerful families in the country: not one was Jewish.

It was true that many Jews had achieved prominence and prosperity in Germany. In 1871, when the Jews had acquired full civil emancipation, and therefore equal opportunity, under the laws, they began entering many new fields of endeavor. It was in the same period that Germany's great industrial and commercial expansion began. Jews, like other Germans, found a ready outlet for their talents. Many became rich or famed as merchants, bankers, manufacturers, publishers, scientists, physicians, lawyers, engineers, musicians, artists, writers. The sudden rise in status made many anti-Semites envious and resentful of the Jews.

A great many German Jews, up until the First World War, felt they were "more German than Jewish." They were confident that cultural assimilation had made them true equals. Jewish liberation, they thought, would last forever. Their contributions to German life were great, but as the historian Peter Gay has noted, "in many respects . . . Germany's Jews remained outsiders. There were still social clubs that would not admit them, private industries that would not employ them, public bodies that would not appoint them. There were fanatics who would not leave them alone."

Jews who converted to Christianity did so for a number of reasons. Whatever the motive, says Professor Gay, "Jews generally despised their baptized brethren as renegades, Christians despised them as opportunists. Converts, seeking to win by moving from one camp to another, lost in both." When Jews refused to assimilate, they were attacked by anti-Semites for being unassimilable. When Jews tried to assimilate, they were accused of debasing or corrupting someone else's culture.

Another charge made by the Nazis was that the German government had been "riddled" with Jews. But in the 19 cabinets of the Weimar Republic, up to 1932, of a total of 237 ministers, only 3 had been Jews; 4 more were described as "of Jewish descent." The last few governments preceding Hitler's had no Jewish ministers. In the federal states the picture was the same.

Documentations of such "innocence" were published by organizations combating anti-Semitism. But it was like trying to stem the cataracts of Niagara with one's hand. Facts were drowned in the ceaseless torrent of anti-Semitic lies.

The truth was the opposite of what Hitler said it was. Rather than an all-powerful threat, the Jews of Europe were the weakest enemy Hitler could have chosen. They had no land of their own, no government, no central authority, no allies, no political weight. They were divided in every possible way. In faith they ranged from devout believers to atheists or converts to Christianity; in income they were rich, poor, and in-between; in politics they included conservatives, liberals, and radicals. If they had been united and highly organized the way the Nazis said they were, then millions more of them might have been saved.

32

The campaign against the Jews began with a pretense of legality. Hitler's measures were introduced one by one. There seems to have been no anti-Jewish program mapped carefully in advance to move from the early step of discrimination to the final step of annihilation. Because the actions taken were sporadic, the effect was to deceive and confuse the Jews. By gradually weakening and demoralizing them, the Nazis were able to reduce resistance and prepare the way for the next, and invariably more terrible, steps. Not until the Holocaust was all over did it become clear that the unbelievable had actually happened. And then people began to say the whole process of destruction had been inevitable from the beginning. They looked back at the steps taken down the long road to death and asked, How could anyone have overlooked the signs?

With the advantage of hindsight, it is not hard to ask that question. But the Jews living through the experience could behave only on the basis of what they knew *then*. The German Jews, the first in Europe to fall victim to Hitler, could reach no real agreement on the nature and extent of the danger threatening them. Nor could they agree on what to do about it. We must realize that there was no historical precedent for the Holocaust. It was a *new* event in world history; the mechanical mass-murder system of an Auschwitz had never happened before. Like any person anywhere, each Jew thought and acted on the basis of his own level of understanding, his own degree of courage, his own moral judgment. For us to evaluate the Jews' actions requires of us that we be able to reconstruct accurately the historical situation which confronted them.

When it was all over, a pattern became clear, of course. First, the Jews were defined and separated from all others; next, everything they owned was stripped from them; then, they were concentrated in ghettos; and finally—extermination.

Nazi propaganda, which had always been fiercely and unrelentingly anti-Semitic, prepared the way for dividing the Jews from the rest of the population. With his party in power, Minister of Propaganda Goebbels had the means to barrage the public daily with complaints and threats against the Jews. The next step was open terror. For a whole week in March 1933, *"Jude verrecke!"* rang through the streets while Storm Troopers beat, robbed, and murdered Jews at will. The police, on orders, stood by and watched. At railway stations, SA bullies met each train, shouting in cadence, "To hell with the Jews!" Nazi thugs stormed into hospitals and courts, ousting Jewish doctors, lawyers, and judges. Then, on April 1, the Nazis sprang the first official governmental act against the Jews—a boycott. SS and SA men picketed Jewish stores, factories, and shops—keeping people from entering. Across shop windows was smeared the word *"Jude."* The Nazi intent was to cut off Jewish enterprises from their customers and suppliers, and thus force the owners to transfer their businesses—cheaply— to non-Jews.

Terror reached into the small towns, too. On Boycott Day in Tienen on the upper Rhine, Storm Troopers paraded through the streets behind a brass band. They set up a firing range—the targets were ugly caricatures of local citizens, labeled "Jew"—and invited the people to practice shooting. At night young men and women caroused in the tavern, bawling out the party anthem, the *"Horst Wessel Lied"*:

> *. . . When Jewish blood spurts from the knife,*
> *Then everything will be fine! . . .*

Driving through the countryside, one could see anti-Jewish posters adorning the entrances and exits of the villages. Shopkeepers posted warnings in their windows: WE DON'T DEAL WITH JEWS.

A week after the boycott, a new law eliminated all "non-Aryans" from civil service and public employment. A "non-Aryan" was any person who had a Jewish parent or Jewish grandparents. In Germany the civil service also included all teaching positions, from the elementary school through university; and most branches of the entertainment industry, including radio, theater, opera, and concerts. About 5,000 Jews lost their jobs. Then came decrees removing all Jews from newspaper staffs and ousting Jews from the guilds which controlled the arts. For a time, Jews holding important jobs in business felt safe, thinking their contracts and their usefulness would save them. But they too were fired. At first, it was by unofficial pressure for "Aryanization"; then, by decree.

Many Jews decided it was time to leave Germany. By the end of the year, over 37,000, about 7 percent of the German Jewish population, had gone abroad to begin new lives.

Still, 1933 was only the beginning. Many Jews (and non-Jews, too) could not believe this barbarism was real. They lived with the illusion that such extreme cruelty could not last much longer —perhaps because it began almost casually, as Maurice Meier describes it. Meier was a Jewish farmer living with his wife Martha and son Ernst near the Swiss border.

> Toward the end of May [1933] Ernst and his schoolmates were looking forward to and making plans for the great day of the school picnic. On the morning of the appointed day Ernst shouldered his rucksack, stuck a spray of blossoms in his hat, and went marching off to school, whistling and full of happy anticipation. About an hour later somebody came and told us that Ernst was standing alone and forlorn on the school grounds. I found him with bloody hands and face, his clothing torn, the contents of the rucksack scattered and trampled in the dust. As he walked home with me he sobbed out his story.
>
> The teacher had read off the names of the pupils who were to go on the picnic, omitting Ernst's name. At the end of the rollcall he looked at Ernst and said, "Jews are not wanted at our picnic." Ernst stepped out of the line and started to walk away, but the teacher shouted to the children, "Boys, get him and knock out of him any ideas he may have about coming to our school anymore." Several rowdies thereupon attacked him, and soon the whole class was scratching, kicking and beating him with the teacher gleefully shouting his encouragement.

The next day Mr. Meier called on the teacher:

> After I had made my complaint he launched into a tirade against the Jews. I then went to the principal. He listened

sympathetically and said, "I am truly sorry for you and for Ernst, but I cannot do a thing because Ernst's teacher is a party member."

"Then what can I do to save the child from such painful experiences?" I asked.

"The only advice I can give you, Herr Meier, is to take Ernst out of school."

This we did, and gave him his lessons at home ourselves.

"Racial science" and "racial culture," as taught in the schools, deeply scarred the young German mind. Erna Listing, a schoolgirl in Gelsenkirchen, was so proud of her essay on the assigned theme, "The Jews Are Our Misfortune," that she sent it to *Der Stürmer*, one of the most violently anti-Semitic newspapers. Appearing in January 1935, it read in part:

> Unfortunately many people today still say, "God created the Jews too. That is why you must respect them also." We say, however, "Vermin are also animals, but we still destroy them." The Jew is a half-caste. He has inherited characteristics of Aryans, Asiatics, Negroes and Mongols. In a half-caste, the worst characteristics predominate. The only good thing about him is his white color. . . .
>
> The Jews have a wicked book of laws. It is called the Talmud. The Jews look on us as animals as well and treat us accordingly. They use cunning tricks to take away our wealth. . . . The Jews have plotted revolts and incited war. They have led Russia into misery. In Germany they gave the Communist Party money and paid their thugs. We were at death's door. Then Adolf Hitler came. Now the Jews are abroad and stir up trouble against us. But we do not waver and we follow the Fuehrer. We do not buy anything from the Jews. Every penny we give them kills one of our own people.
>
> Heil Hitler!

Not until 1935 did Hitler make anti-Semitism part of Germany's basic legal code. On September 15, he introduced the

Nuremberg Laws. They dealt with "Citizenship" and the "Protection of German Blood and German Honor." Under these laws the Jews were deprived of their political rights. They were no longer citizens; they were reduced to subjects. Mixed marriages and extramarital sex relations between Jews and Aryans were made criminal offenses. The Nazis simply legalized the terror that had preceded the laws and went ahead to erect, on the foundation of the Nuremberg Laws, a structure of new decrees which robbed the Jews of their last remaining rights.

A quota system had already reduced the number of Jews in higher education to the proportion of Jews in the population. Now came a decree expelling all Jews from German schools. (Jews could then attend Jewish schools only.) The segregation of Jews extended to sleepers and dining cars on all railway lines, then to waiting rooms and rest rooms in all railway stations. Special shopping hours for Jews were introduced, limiting them to one or two hours a day. Beaches, resorts, and public baths were declared off limits to Jews. Jews could not have their hair cut in Aryan barbershops or get medical care in Aryan hospitals. A curfew was ordered: all Jews had to be off the streets after 8:00 P.M. Jews could not use trolleys and buses in rush hours and could sit only when there were no Aryan standees. Non-Aryan cars were assigned "Jew numbers" for their license plates. Private telephones were ripped out of Jewish apartments, and Jews were denied the use of public phones. Even before ghetto districts were set up, there was a period when Jews could live only in those houses marked for Jews.

The Nuremberg Laws and their thirteen supplementary decrees were nothing new, the German government claimed. Hitler was simply restoring the conditions of the era before Emancipation. As one Nazi spokesman put it, "It will henceforth and for all future times be impossible for the Jews to mix with the German people and to meddle in the political, economic, and cultural management of the Reich."

These restrictions—so like the old slave codes and Jim Crow laws that afflicted Black Americans for centuries—were reinforced by identification measures. As in any police state, identification documents were vital. Jews had to carry ID cards and to show them in all dealings with Party and government offices. German passports held by Jews were stamped with a big, red capital "J." When rationing began, the same "J" was printed on the ration cards of Jews. Even a Jew's name could no longer be his or her own choice. Jews who had taken German names had to go back to their old names. In addition, Jewish men had to use the middle name "Israel"; and Jewish women, the middle name "Sarah." The imposed names had to be recorded on all birth and marriage certificates.

Then came the stamping of Jewish identification on the person and the home. Jews six years of age or over were ordered to wear a Jewish star in public. It had to be a black star on a yellow background, big as the palm of the hand and sewn over the left breast of the clothing. In the center of every star, the word "Jude." Later, Jews were ordered to paste a paper star on their doors, too.

The labeling of Jews was a viciously effective weapon. It helped the Nazis monitor residence and movement. It made it easy for the police to pick up Jews anywhere at any time. And it had a crippling effect on the victims. Jews felt naked before their enemies. The whole world was watching them. To hide, to escape, to resist meant ridding oneself of badge, middle name, ID papers. But to do that was a serious crime, and there were spies and informers everywhere to recognize and denounce a Jew. Yet to go on wearing the star—what could it mean but disaster, death?

In the beginning, the Jews of Germany had no central organization to turn to for help. Each city had its own Jewish administrative group, which took care of Jewish schools, hospitals, and synagogues. A few months after Nazism took over, these groups began planning a national organization. Called the Representative Council of Jews in Germany, it began work late in 1933, under the chairmanship of Rabbi Leo Baeck of Berlin. Its original purpose was political, not financial. It sought open debate with the Nazis on anti-Semitism and the future of Germany's Jews. But Hitler listened to no one else's opinion. And so, the organization found it more and more essential to provide relief, care for the sick, schooling for the children, and opportunities for emigration.

The anti-Semitic program proved useful in mobilizing the country for total war. While ridding Germany of Jews, Hitler was training the Germans in the brutality needed to gain domination over all of Europe. The violence and corruption typical of the Nazis before they came to power now became endemic to Germany. It was known that Count Helldorf, head of Berlin's police force, had developed an enormously profitable racket out of the Jews' desperate desire to escape abroad. He would seize their passports, then sell them back at the highest possible price. They paid it. No price was too high if it was liberty one was buying. Bribery became so highly organized, it seemed legal to everyone.

As for violence, the German people became so accustomed to it that even the children practiced it casually. Bella Fromm, the Berlin journalist, jotted down this scene in her diary for June 1, 1938:

> Driving out to Potsdam, I came across a group of youngsters, dressed in the Hitler Youth outfit, beating up a skinny, undersized, fair boy. I stopped.
> "Aren't you ashamed, eight big strong fellows like you, jumping on a six-year-old?"
> The oldest of the gang explained. "We discovered that this dirty swine was nothing but a Jewish bastard. He refused to answer the Heil Hitler salute, and said he was Jewish. So we took his pants off to find out whether he is circumcised."

On June 28, Fromm was alerted by a friend in the Foreign Office that a pogrom had been organized for that day in Berlin. She went out on the streets to observe:

> The entire Kurfürstendamm was plastered with scrawls and cartoons. "Jew" was smeared all over the doors, windows and walls in waterproof colors. It grew worse as we came to the part of town where poor little Jewish retail shops were to be

found. The SA had created havoc. Everywhere were revolting and bloodthirsty pictures of Jews beheaded, hanged, tortured, and maimed, accompanied by obscene inscriptions. Windows were smashed, and loot from the miserable little shops was strewn over the sidewalk and floating in the gutter.

We were just about to enter a tiny jewelry shop when a gang of ten youngsters in Hitler Youth uniforms smashed the show window and stormed into the shop, brandishing butcher knives and yelling: "To hell with the Jewish rabble! Room for the Sudeten Germans!"

The smallest boy of the mob climbed inside the window and started his work of destruction by flinging everything he could grab right into the streets. Inside, the other boys broke glass shelves and counters, hurling alarm clocks, cheap silverware, and trifles to their accomplices outside. A tiny shrimp of a boy crouched in a corner of the window, putting dozens of rings on his fingers and stuffing his pockets with wristwatches and bracelets. His uniform bulging with loot, he turned around, spat squarely into the shopkeeper's face, and dashed off.

The little old Jew kept his poise and tried to reassure us. "I am only glad that my wife died ten days ago. God spared her this ordeal. We have been starving for a long time. Business was dead. The law prevents us from getting out of a lease or dismissing an employee as long as a penny can be squeezed out."

Bella Fromm was worried about two old friends whom she had helped with money and food during the last two years. They had lost their two sons—killed for Germany!—during the First World War. She went to find out whether they had suffered:

Their shop was in ruins. Their goods, paper and stationery, trampled into the gutter. Three SA men, roaring with obscene laughter, forced the trembling old man to pick up the broken glass with hands that were covered with blood. We stood there, choking with rage, trembling in horror, impotent and helpless.

The next day, when we returned to bring them food and see what else we could do to help them, we found two coffins surrounded by silent neighbors. The faces of the old couple seemed peaceful and serene amid the broken glass and destruction. As we put down our baskets and stood there wretchedly, a young woman spoke to me. "It is better for them. They took poison last night."

Making what would be her last trip through Germany before emigrating to America, Bella Fromm came across a sight that crystallized everything she had experienced in these first six years of Hitlerism. In Frankfurt they had changed the *Paul Ehrlich Strasse* into *Heinrich Himmler Strasse*. "The man who saved humanity by his cure for syphilis," she wrote, "has been replaced by a sadistic butcher."

5

Flight—to Nowhere

Stripped of citizenship, rights, work, property, dignity, the Jews of Germany had only one hope: emigration. By the end of 1937, nearly 130,000 Jews had taken that course. But three-quarters of Germany's Jews still remained inside Hitler's borders. As they scrambled frantically to find a way out, the Jewish leader Chaim Weizmann spoke prophetically of the fate of all of Europe's Jews:

> Today almost six million Jews are doomed to be pent up
> in places where they are not wanted, and for whom the world
> is divided into places where they cannot live, and places into
> which they cannot enter.

Hitler did not want the Jews. Get rid of them, he told his officials. His policy still seemed to be expulsion, not extermination. But as he moved closer to war, the possibility of flight for the Jews narrowed. And the possibility of extermination widened.

Late in 1937 Hitler confided to a few trusted military and political leaders that he planned to take over Austria and then Czechoslovakia. If it took war to achieve his goals, Germany must be ready for it. His successes at home and abroad had given him a monumental confidence in his own infallibility. In the spring of 1936 he had remilitarized the Rhineland, illegally, and no one had acted to stop him. That summer of 1936 he had played host to the world at the Olympic Games in Berlin, and no one had refused to take part. For two years now his troops and planes had been helping Franco to destroy the Spanish Republic, and the West had stayed "neutral."

Now in March 1938, he took over Austria while everyone watched and no one interfered. The Nazis set up a Jewish emigration center in Vienna in April. And Adolf Eichmann, one of Heydrich's civil servants, was put in charge. Eichmann had joined the Nazi party in 1932, after a short career as a traveling salesman for an oil company. As a young Nazi hopeful, he behaved like the typical bureaucrat, doing exactly what he was told and getting little recognition for it. Until he saw, in this movement powered by a raging anti-Semitism, his chance to advance by becoming an "expert" on Jewish affairs. By 1938 he was head of the SD unit called "Jewry." And now he had his first big job in Vienna.

In one year, by combining terror and blackmail with the threat of concentration camps, he deported 100,000 Jews, almost half the total number in Austria. He saw himself as a disciplined technician, providing an "objective" solution to the Jewish problem. "Each of us," he said later, "as an individual had no wish to harm the Jews individually."

But what could Eichmann do with the hundreds of thousands of Jews still in Germany and Austria? The refugee problem came to a head, for as the cry for help swelled, the chance to escape grew slimmer. A High Commission for Refugees from Germany had been established by the League of Nations. But so little willingness to help was displayed by the member nations that the commissioner, James MacDonald, resigned in protest.

In July 1938, at the request of President Franklin D. Roosevelt, 32 nations met at Evian, France, to see what refuge they could offer to the persecuted Jews. Just before the conference, on Hitler's orders, the synagogues of Munich, Nuremberg, and Dortmund were destroyed, and mass arrests of Jews were made. The delegations came up with no proposals, nor did they even show any indignation over Nazi policy. In a week the conference closed. No country was willing to change its policy for the Jews.

That September at Munich, Hitler frightened England and

France into signing a pact that sacrificed Czechoslovakia. That Republic, created by peace treaties after the First World War, was made up of several nationalities, among them the Germans of the Sudetenland region. Concealing his true aim—to destroy the Czech state and grab its territory and people for the Third Reich —Hitler threatened war unless his outrageous claim upon the Sudetenland was satisfied. He assured the British and French, who had pledged to defend Czechoslovakia from attack, that the Sudetenland was his final territorial demand in Europe. The gullible British Prime Minister, Neville Chamberlain, took Hitler's word. Czechoslovakia, deserted by her allies, fell into Hitler's hands. Such futile attempts to appease an insatiable appetite for power and territory came to be known as the "Munich spirit." People everywhere foolishly gave thanks that "peace in our time" was assured.

When the Western powers failed to support Czechoslovakia against Hitler, Heydrich took it as a signal that he could dump Jews upon the smaller nations without fear of reprisals. Toward the end of October, thousands of Polish Jews living in Germany were served deportation notices. Roused from their beds at night, 12,000 Jews, taking only what they could carry, were bundled into freight cars, forced across the Polish border, and dumped into a freezing no-man's-land. Many of the old and sick died of exposure. The others, through the efforts of the American Joint Distribution Committee (JDC), were finally quartered in Polish towns.

By the end of 1938, it was clear to Hitler that emigration alone would not solve his "Jewish problem." There were still too many Jews in Reich territory. A Foreign Office memo complained that "almost every state in the world has . . . hermetically sealed its borders against these parasitical Jewish intruders. . . ."

Eichmann, however, kept trying to get rid of Jews. In July 1939 he set up another emigration center in Prague, and announced that 70,000 Jews would be deported within a year. The Jewish Community Council of the city was told to provide daily quotas of Jews and the funds to pay for their emigration. Jews were ordered to leave the Czech provinces and to gather in Prague. But once there, where could they be deported? Those with property negotiated their own exits with the Gestapo; the poorer Jews were stranded.

What was the rest of the world doing to help the desperate Jews? The United States let in about 100,000 Jewish refugees until 1939, the outbreak of the Second World War. (It was less than 2 percent of America's small Jewish population.) Few as they were, their entrance was resisted by many Americans. It was hard for Europe's beleaguered Jews to understand why. They had thought of President Roosevelt as their friend. His New Deal government was certainly humane. But though he spoke often and sympathetically of the plight of the persecuted Jews, his administration did little to help them. Some people argued that to bring in more refugees during the Great Depression would add to the nation's problems. Others claimed it would be taken as interference with another nation's internal affairs. Some said it would force changes in the immigration quota system, which they did not want to make. And, when the war came, some said, it would hurt the defense effort.

The terrible truth was that in ten crucial years, 1933–1943, there were over 400,000 unfilled places within United States immigration quotas for refugees from countries under Hitler's rule. Each place unfilled was a sentence of death for a European Jew.

The non-Nazi countries of Europe took about 150,000 refugees. England accepted the largest number, 80,000; France, about 25,000; Holland, 22,000; Belgium, 13,000; Switzerland, 9,000.

About 40,000 refugees found homes in Latin America. Half went to Argentina, and the remainder dispersed to other countries in South and Central America and the West Indies. But by the end of 1938, Latin America banged the door shut. In 1939 Japanese-occupied Shanghai, China, became the haven for 10,000 Jews. It was a free port that put up no bar to refugees, except that they could not move into the interior of China.

Other than the United States, Palestine was the most practical goal of emigrating Jews, but it, too, put up entry restrictions. The policy of the British, who controlled the Middle East, was concerned with Arabs as well as Jews. If war with Hitler should come, the support of the Jews was inevitable. But not that of the Arabs. So the British Mandate for Palestine, which provided for facilitating Jewish emigration "under suitable conditions," was interpreted to suit imperial, not humane, policies. The British allowed entry to Jews with a certain amount of money, but all others were restricted. Then, in its White Paper of May 1939, the British Colonial Office took steps to end Jewish entry into Palestine. It was to be permitted for only another five years, at the rate of 10,000 per year. To help meet the immediate crisis, an additional 25,000 people were to be allowed in if their maintenance could be guaranteed. The result was that only about 70,000 refugees entered Palestine up until 1941. All hope of escape was denied to the millions of Jews the war would trap in Eastern Europe.

(The Arabs, it should be noted, failed to defend British interests during World War II. Instead, they allied themselves with Hitler. The Jews of Palestine—what other choice did they have?—fought alongside the British wherever they could.)

How could Jews leave Hitler's Reich if there was no place for them to go? By this time Jews would pay any price and undergo any danger to escape Nazism. A new "travel trade" sprang up, a racket that police and ministry officials manipulated. The market for exporting Jews was lively, and Nazis (and many others) could make fat profits at every stage of the deadly game. As the pressure increased, the number who could find a route of escape diminished to a lucky few. One of those routes was via water. It was an enormously complex task to organize a rescue by ship. An available vessel had to be located; money raised to buy it and put a crew aboard; smugglers paid to sneak refugees to the port; and officials bribed to close their eyes to illegalities. To finance the steamship fares, dollars were almost always demanded, a transaction the American Joint Distribution Committee (JDC) organized through a special bureau.

And after all this, there was never any guarantee that the ship would sail, or if it did, that it would reach a safe harbor.

The story of the voyage of the *St. Louis* is but one such

episode. The ship left Hamburg, Germany, in May 1939, bound for Havana, Cuba. Aboard were 937 Jewish passengers, all with American quota permits and special permits to wait in Cuba while their American visas were being processed. But when they reached Havana, a presidential decree had made their permits worthless. The ship cruised aimlessly in the Atlantic, waiting for some government to save the despairing passengers. Finally, after thirty-five days at sea, England, France, Holland, and Belgium agreed to share the human cargo. But many other ships were ordered back when country after country refused to accept refugees.

The *Struma*, a broken-down cattle boat, carried 769 Rumanian Jews to Istanbul, Turkey, where they were to be given visas for Palestine. But the Turks sent them back; the ship suddenly sank in the Black Sea; and all the refugees but one drowned.

The ancient paddle-wheel steamer, the *Pentcho*, took aboard 511 Jews fleeing from Central Europe, hoping to reach Palestine. Down the Danube they sailed on the rickety, leaking boat, past one country after another which refused to let them come in for food and water. After weeks aboard, the refugees were filthy and starving. Many jumped overboard to swim ashore, but they were forced back. It took almost five months to reach the Black Sea. With no lifeboats, no life preservers, and no radio, the ship began a wild, aimless journey among the Greek Islands. Then one day the boiler exploded, and the engine stopped. Bunk sheets were gathered, and the women sewed them up into sails. A storm drove the *Pentcho* onto the rocks of an uninhabited island in the Aegean Sea. The passengers managed to scramble ashore and watched the ship break into pieces and sink. Scouring the island for food, they could find no birds, no animals, and no fresh water. Eleven terrible days passed. Then an Italian warship rescued them, only to put them into a concentration camp on the island of Rhodes. There they stayed for a year and a half, until finally they were sent to Italy, only, once more, to be penned up in a concentration camp.

BOOK TWO

Destruction
of the Jews

6

The Night of Broken Glass

On November 7, 1938, a seventeen-year-old boy, Herschel Grynszpan, walked up to the German embassy in Paris and shot to death one of its minor staff, Ernst vom Rath.

Young Herschel was the son of one of the 12,000 Jews of Polish origin who a few days earlier had been deported from Germany to Poland. Herschel's father had lived in Germany for twenty-seven years. Like many such immigrants, he had never bothered to seek naturalization. Now, overnight, his life had been senselessly smashed.

When Herschel, in Paris visiting an uncle, got a postcard telling of his father's deportation, the act of murder followed. Exactly why the boy did it or what he hoped to achieve by it has never been clear. But the consequences were catastrophic.

The assassination triggered a nationwide pogrom (massacre) in Germany on the night of November 9, the *Kristallnacht* (Night of Broken Glass), which foreshadowed the extermination of the Jews. The assault had been planned by Heydrich and Goebbels at the first news of the shooting of vom Rath. Nazi regional chiefs were instructed by teletype to destroy Jewish shops, synagogues, businesses, and homes. The police were not to interfere, except to protect Aryan life and property. Jews, especially rich ones, were to be arrested and confined in concentration camps.

The Party carried out its orders. The torch was set to most of Germany's synagogues; 7,500 shops were ransacked and many destroyed; and hundreds of homes were looted and wrecked. Damage to property, equipment, and stock was estimated at several hundred million marks. At least 1,000 Jews were murdered, and 26,000 were flung into concentration camps.

An American eyewitness described what he saw in Leipzig that night:

> Jewish dwellings were smashed into and the contents demolished or looted. In one of the Jewish sections, an eighteen-year-old boy was hurled from a three-story window to land with both legs broken on a street littered with burning beds and other household furniture. . . . Jewish shop windows by the hundreds were systematically and wantonly smashed throughout the city at a loss estimated at several millions of marks. . . . The main streets of the city were a positive litter of shattered plate glass. . . . The debacle was executed by SS men and Storm Troopers, not in uniform, each group having been provided with hammers, axes, crowbars and incendiary bombs. . . .

A fourteen-year-old boy, M. I. Libau, had gone to bed that night in his home in Berlin. Suddenly, at six o'clock in the morning, the doorbell rang, waking him up. His mother went to the door and opened it. He told what happened then:

> I heard the shrill, barking, yelling voices of men. It seemed to me there were at least twenty.
> "Are here Gojim or Iwrim [Gentiles or Jews]?" Then I heard my mother's calm voice. "Please speak German. I understand it very well, but if you wish to know whether we are Christians or Jews, we are Jews!"
> "Where are the Jews? Where are they?" they yelled. I heard noises of falling furniture and breaking glass. I could not imagine what was happening. I stood behind my bed when one Nazi in full uniform entered the room. He stepped back a fraction of a second when he saw me; then he began to yell, "I'll do nothing to you. I won't do any harm to you."

Now he stood near me, his face sweating. A smell of bad alcohol came out of his mouth. He took another glaring look at me and began to destroy everything within reach. While he was breaking the closet door, my mother came into the room. He commanded her to hold the clothes for him so that he would be able to tear them better. Desperately my mother called out, "Those are all our clothes! What shall we wear?"

"You wear? Nothing!" he shouted. "You don't need any more clothes! You can go naked now."

It almost broke my heart when I saw him take my father's best suit. "This is my father's best suit," I called out. "Don't tear it! Don't!"

. . . We watched the men destroy the whole apartment of five rooms. All the things for which my parents had worked for eighteen long years were destroyed in less than ten minutes. Piles of valuable glasses, expensive furniture, linens—in short, everything was destroyed; nothing was left untouched. After those ten minutes, the apartment was a heap of ruins.

My mother and I looked at everything without shedding a tear. We felt as if we had lost our minds. The Nazis left us, yelling, "Don't try to leave this house! We'll soon be back again and take you to concentration camp to be shot."

But the Nazis did not come back—then. Mr. Libau, who had been working nights as a forced laborer on the railroad, came home and went into hiding in the cellar of a Christian friend. Many of the family's friends committed suicide that night, some went insane, and some were murdered.

In cold, precise detail, like a bookkeeper's account, the leader of the SS in the town of Geldern reported the action taken locally on orders he had received by telephone:

The first measure was the setting on fire of the synagogue in Geldern at about 4 A.M. By 9 A.M. this was burned down to the foundations. Some bibles in Hebrew characters were taken into safekeeping. Simultaneously the interior fittings of the synagogue in Xanten (a private house) were completely destroyed.

53

There existed two Jewish shops in the Sturm district, the fittings and small stock of which were likewise completely destroyed.

The furnishings of the remainder of the Jews, former cattle-Jews and now earning their living by private means, were totally demolished and rendered unusable, the windows and windowpanes first having been broken in. . . .

By about 11 hours [11 A.M.] all the male Jews fifteen to seventy years of age were arrested by the police and kept temporarily in the local guardhouses. . . . The population took a passive attitude to the demonstrators. . . .

Making a secret report on Nazi party members who had murdered Jews that night, the chief Party judge, Major Walter Buch, revealed how justice had disappeared in Hitler's Germany:

In the following cases of killing Jews, proceedings were suspended or minor punishments were pronounced: Party Member Fruehling, August, because of shooting of the Jewish couple Goldberg and because of shooting of the Jew Simasohm . . . Party Members Behring, Willi and Heike, Josef, because of shooting of the Jew Rosenbaum and the Jewess Zwienicki . . . Party Members Schmidt, Heinrich, and Meckler, Ernst, because of drowning of the Jew Ilsoffer . . . etc. etc. etc.

Why the *Kristallnacht* pogroms at this moment? Earlier, if they had wished, the Nazis could have invented any pretext to commit the same barbarism. But not until now did Hitler feel secure enough to dare a crime of this magnitude. He had learned he need fear no opposition from Germans or from the world outside.

Kristallnacht was still another measure of how far Hitler would go. Coming immediately after his successful intimidation of the major powers at Munich, it tested the German spirit. If his people could swallow this, they could swallow anything. Was any voice raised in protest? Neither the Catholic nor the Protestant

Church offered sanctuary to the stricken Jews. Hitler could smile comfortably and say, "My Germans are united behind me."

There were notable exceptions. One Catholic churchman, Bernard Lichtenberg, Provost of Saint Hedwig's Cathedral in Berlin, spoke out from the pulpit the morning after the pogrom:

> What took place yesterday, we know; what will be tomorrow, we do not know; but what happens today, that we have witnessed; outside, the synagogue is burning, and that, also, is a house of God. . . .
>
> In a number of Berlin homes, an anonymous inflammatory rag against the Jews is being distributed. It says that any German who, from allegedly false sentimentality, helps the Jews, commits treason against his own people. Do not let yourself be led astray by such unChristian thoughts, but act according to the clear command of Christ: "Thou shalt love thy neighbor as thyself."

Because Father Lichtenberg spoke, he served two years in prison. Released, he was seized by the Gestapo and sent to Dachau. He died on the way.

Far more true to the feelings of German Christians at the time was the action of *Landesbischof* Weidemann of Bremen; on November 28, shortly after the burning, pillaging, imprisonment, and murder of the Jews throughout Germany, the state bishop sent this telegram:

TO: THE FUEHRER AND REICHSCHANCELLOR ADOLF HITLER

THE THREE CHURCHES OF GRATITUDE IN BREMEN HAVE BEEN INAUGURATED. THEY BEAR YOUR NAME, MEIN FÜHRER, IN GRATITUDE TO GOD FOR THE MIRACULOUS REDEMPTION OF OUR NATION AT YOUR HANDS FROM THE ABYSS OF JEWISH-MATERIALISTIC BOLSHEVISM. I THANK YOU FOR HAVING ENABLED US TO EXPRESS IN THESE NEW CHURCHES WHAT IS A DEEP CONFESSION FOR US WHO ARE FULLY CONSCIOUS CHRISTIAN NATIONAL SOCIALISTS.

HEIL, MEIN FÜHRER!

The pogroms of *Kristallnacht* were the unofficial penalty for the death of vom Rath. The next day, Hitler decided to demand the collective punishment of all the Jews. The Fuehrer told Goering that the "Jewish question" must be "coordinated and solved, now, once and for all, in one way or another."

The German bureaucracy swung into action. Measures against the Jews would be planned in an orderly, legal, and systematic way. Pogroms were too messy. The mob turned loose could not always be controlled: *Kristallnacht* had done harm to non-Jewish property and had cost the state some losses. No more. The experts would confer; decisions would be scientifically made; the proper directives would be issued; the necessary reports made out and filed.

When casual violence on the streets stopped, many Jews were fooled into believing the worst was over. But it was not; terror simply took another form. Goering imposed the huge fine of 1 billion marks on the Jews; it was the value of 20 percent of all their remaining property. Two billion marks had already been taken from the Jews. The government had collected this "Atonement Payment" and poured it into the rearmament program. Compulsory Aryanization of Jewish businesses moved ahead rapidly. By the year's end, what was left of Jewish business and self-employment was wiped out. It is worth noting that such steps taken "for the good of the German people" at first benefited only one class—the owners of Aryan enterprises. Later the state pocketed a part of the loot.

Before the time of *Kristallnacht*, about a quarter of the Jewish population of Germany had emigrated. A year later, more than half the Jews were gone. Three-quarters of those who remained were older people—their businesses, savings, professions, jobs, all gone. They were a dependent community badly in need of relief. It was now that the SD took over the Representative Council of Jews, converted it into the Reich Association of Jews in Germany, and made membership for all "racial" Jews compulsory. It was the equivalent of a Nazi-controlled ghetto. Public relief was denied the Jews. Unemployed Jews were put to hard labor on construction and reclamation projects, or in arms plants. Jewish wages were slashed, and what was left, taxed. It was slave labor.

"But," said Heydrich, "in spite of the elimination of the Jews from economic life, the main problem remains, namely, to kick the Jew out of Germany."

7

A Prophecy

Today I will once more be a prophet! If the international Jewish financiers inside and outside Europe should again succeed in plunging the nations into a world war, the result will be not the bolshevization of the earth and thus the victory of Jewry, but the annihilation of the Jewish race throughout Europe.

This was Hitler's voice, speaking to the Reichstag on January 30, 1939. His prophecy of annihilation for the Jews came only seven months before he himself would plunge the nations into the war of conquest he had been planning from the day he took power.

Did he predict annihilation because he knew his policy of mass deportation was coming to an end? Through "voluntary" emigration he had already driven out half the Jews of Germany, and brought the remainder to mass destitution. On September 1, 1939, he took the step which would lead to the destruction of the Jews of Europe. Germany attacked Poland.

The blame for starting World War II rests solely on Nazi Germany. It would be hard to find a historian who disagrees. The deeper roots of that war may be tangled and hard to trace, but one cause was Hitler's desire to see his "superior" Germans rule mankind. More important, argues historian Lucy Dawidowicz, was Hitler's conception of the war as a means to reach the Jews of Europe and annihilate them.

Back in November 1937, Hitler had secretly told his military leaders of his plans for the war. The only question for Germany, he said, is where the greatest possible conquest could be made at lowest cost. By a policy of international blackmail, and without firing a shot, he had already taken the Rhineland, Austria, and Czechoslovakia. When he sent his armies smashing through Poland, he scrapped the pact he had made at Munich assuring the West that Germany's territorial ambitions were satisfied. "In starting and making a war," he said, "it is not right that matters, but victory."

He began the war with the brute desire to exploit the people and the resources of the territories he would conquer. Everything that could be used by the German war economy was to be ripped away from Poland, and the Poles were to be made the "slaves of the Greater German World Empire." He had no plans to remake Poland, only to destroy it.

In scarcely three weeks most of the fighting was over. The new German army moved with a speed, efficiency, and ruthlessness that astonished and terrified the world. (Six months later Hitler conquered Denmark and Norway. Then Holland, Belgium, and France fell to the German army's *Blitzkrieg* [onslaught]. Only Britain was left in the West.)

The German soldiers entering Poland saw themselves as heroes of the "master race"; their victims, the Poles, were *Untermenschen*, subhumans. And the Jews among them were an even lower category—bacilli. In 1939 there were 3.3 million Jews in Poland—10 percent of the total population. About a third lived in the countryside, and two-thirds, in towns and cities. Two million Jews fell directly into Hitler's hands in the invasion. The others came under Russian control when Stalin (under the pact he had signed with Hitler in August 1939) invaded Poland from the other side. The two powers divided the country between themselves, and Poland, as a state, ceased to exist.

On September 21, Heydrich issued his plan for Poland's Jews.

First, they would be concentrated in ghettos. Jews would be removed from the countryside and its villages, and forced into ghettos in the larger cities. Councils of Jewish Elders would be set up to administer the segregated communities. Later, it would turn out that the ghettos were way stations to the death camps, and the Councils were not the traditional councils of Jewish self-government but Nazi instruments for extermination.

Who were the Jews of Eastern Europe? There were 7 million of them living in that huge territory bounded by Germany on the west, the Dnieper River on the east, the Baltic Sea on the north, and the Black Sea on the south. Their settlement in Eastern Europe had started in the thirteenth century, with people from Bohemia and Germany. The Jews expelled from the West during the next centuries headed in many directions, but large numbers of them settled in the East. They were welcomed by the Polish rulers for the help they could give in the crucial task of building the country's economy. By 1500, the center of the Jewish world had moved east of the Rhine. Their lot in the Middle Ages, contrasted with the horrors of Western Europe, was not unbearable.

But the good life did not last long. Soon the epidemic of religious hatred and violence reached into the East too, and the effect was catastrophic. Living conditions became as intolerable for Jews in Poland, Lithuania, the Ukraine, and Galicia as they were in the other Christian countries. Church laws forced Jews into ghettos and branded them with the yellow badge. In the seventeenth century, a Ukrainian uprising wiped out hundreds of Jewish communities, and hundreds of thousands—a third of the Jewish population—died by the sword, famine, and pestilence. Repeated pogroms left deep wounds in the consciousness of East European Jews, wounds which succeeding generations never healed.

When Poland was swallowed up by Russia, Prussia, and Austria after the defeat of Napoleon, a huge mass of Jews came under czarist rule. To keep the Jews out of the interior, the czar mapped out a region all Jews were forced to live in—the Pale of Settlement. The Jews were allowed their traditional right of self-government in religious affairs, but the state restricted every other aspect of life. Hundreds of anti-Jewish laws and regulations were applied mercilessly. No matter what czar sat on the throne, the persecution of the Jews continued. Anti-Semitism was like an official faith, observed and respected everywhere in the Russian Empire.

In the 1870s, pogroms engineered by the government began to break out. Within a decade, new anti-Jewish restrictions and disabilities were piled upon the old. Under these crushing blows, 1⅓ million Jews fled the Empire between 1881 and 1918. Most settled in the United States, but many went to Western Europe and elsewhere. More would have escaped if they had had the means. But the mass of East European Jews were desperately poor. Most were factory workers, artisans, and petty tradespeople who worked fifteen and more hours a day and lived on a diet of potatoes and herring.

They lived largely in the shtetls of Eastern Europe, the thousands of small towns scattered throughout the Pale of Settlement. The shtetls were essentially marketplaces for trading goods and services. The little towns were islands in a sea of poor, illiterate peasants. The Jews lived a separate life as a minority within the culture of the majority. During World War I, the Jews fell victim to both sides as the fighting moved back and forth. They were arrested, tortured, deported, massacred. Out of that war came the birth of Poland as an independent state. But it did not bring the Jews a better life. Not even to the small number of assimilationist Jews, who came from the wealthy families. These "Poles of Mosaic faith," as they called themselves, stressed their deep bonds with the Polish nation and their distinctness from the Orthodox Jews. In their own eyes they were really Poles, not Jews. (Didn't the assimilationist Jews of Germany think the same way?) But the Poles didn't believe the Jews were Poles. Poland, like Nazi Germany, defined the Jews as a race. The Poles thought of the Jews as a strange people, a foreign people, a hostile people. And the very fact that assimilationist Jews were especially prominent among the leading scientists, artists, and writers made them highly suspect to the Poles. No matter how they talked, looked, or behaved—no matter what medals they wore or what contributions they made to Polish culture—Jews they were and Jews they would remain. Only, unlike the other Jews, these were enemies in disguise.

The assimilationist Jews did not join political movements which offered nationalist solutions to the problems of anti-Semitism. They rejected both the Zionists and the Bundists, who fought for the right of Jews to live as a distinct people. The Zionists, with whose aims perhaps 40 percent of the Polish Jews sympathized, saw the goal as a return to the national homeland in Palestine. The Bund, which was the socialist organization to which most of the Jewish workers belonged, believed a revolution in Poland would give the Jews freedom and national equality. Only some 20 percent of all Polish Jews were "still dominated by a religious mentality" at this time, according to the historian Reuben Ainsztein.

The great majority of Jews supported Polish freedom, hoping for recognition as a national minority and for equal rights. But most Polish political parties opposed those demands. Pogroms broke out the very day Polish independence was proclaimed. And from that time on, robberies, beatings, and murders of Jews were everyday events. Poland earned a worldwide reputation as a state where national minorities were oppressed and persecuted. Although Jewish deputies were elected to the Polish parliament, they never succeeded in winning enough support to protect Jewish interests. The ancient anti-Semitism continued, fueled now by the rise of new fascist parties and anti-Jewish groups.

In the depression of the 1930s, anti-Semitic violence raged through the universities and the provincial towns. A new slogan appeared everywhere: "There is no place for Jews in Poland." The government-supported press was peppered with articles treating the Jews as an inevitable evil. In despair, the Jewish press forecast a "catastrophe for Polish Jewry." In 1935 a new Polish constitution abolished parliamentary democracy and replaced it with a fascist system. Nazi racial theories and practices were adopted. Plans were made to force mass Jewish emigration.

But most countries discriminated against Jewish immigrants. Only 117,000 Jews were able to leave Poland in the years between 1931 and 1938. Anti-Jewish riots broke out in many cities and towns. Jewish people were attacked, stores looted, tradespeople barred from markets and fairs. When a delegation of Polish Jews called on the head of the government's Nationalities Department to ask that steps be taken against anti-Semitic propaganda, he replied:

> Nowadays everybody in Poland is anti-Semitic. We cannot assign police to protect every single Jew. We do not intend, moreover, to hang young people just for being anti-Semitic.

Knowing that the government would not protect Jews, the Bund, as early as 1920, had organized its own self-defense force. The small but permanent militia guarded not only the Bund, its members, headquarters, and street demonstrations, but Jews in general. It countered violence with violence.

Although the use of physical force had been regarded by many as alien to Jewish character and tradition, the Bund concluded that self-defense was not only necessary now, but honorable and heroic. And when violence had to be used, the Bund—through the trained and armed militia of both its adult and youth groups —used it to good effect. During a general strike called to protest a pogrom of 1936, a Bund leader, Z. Artur, declared:

> Today the Jewish working class is saying to the fascist and anti-Semitic hooligans: the time has passed when Jews could be subjected to pogroms with impunity. There exists a mass of workers raised in the Bund tradition of struggle and self-defense. With them one can wage war, but not pogroms that remain unpunished.

One day the Polish Foreign Minister announced that Poland had room for barely half a million Jews. The rest of them, he said, had better get out.

By 1938 the Polish government was coordinating its policy

with Nazi Germany's. But that confidence in Hitler as an ally was terribly misplaced. It led to a catastrophe for Poland itself, as well as for the Jews.

From the first day of Hitler's invasion, the massacre began. The *Einsatzgruppen*—the "mobile killing units" of the SS, under the command of Reinhard Heydrich—moved into Poland with the regular armored columns. Their instructions were to kill as many civilians as possible, especially Jews. Masses of Jews were now condemned to death, although at this point it was not yet clear that Hitler planned total extermination. He would use three basic methods for his "Final Solution of the Jewish Question": starvation, shooting, and, in the end, gassing. The *Einsatzgruppen's* weapon was the gun. (Later it became the gas van.) The troops were drafted from the Armed SS, and their commanders were chosen by Heydrich from the SS elite having academic degrees. Most were professional men—teachers, artists, lawyers, a physician, even a clergyman—and most were in their thirties. No one was asked to volunteer, but once chosen, they did their job of mass murder with zeal and skill.

There were four of these mobile killing units, each of battalion size, totaling about 3,000 men. Operating in different zones of Eastern Europe, they worked closely with the regular armed forces, which handed over captured Jews and often lent their own men to assist in the massacres. In addition, the killing units were aided by more than 200,000 eager collaborators from the local populations. Historian Raul Hilberg estimates they murdered 1.4 million Jews by the end of the war. One officer alone, Dr. Otto Bradfisch, handled the killing of at least 15,000 people. Another, Dr. Otto Ohlendorf, a research economist, directed the killing of 90,000 Jews.

Death did not always come swiftly at the hands of the killing squads. Before the bullet there was often barbarous cruelty, details of which the SS liked to photograph and send home. In town after town—Bielsko, Kalisz, Wloclawek, Mielec, Wieruszow, Zgierz, Aleksandrovsk, Piotrkow, Lukow—the horrors mounted. The conquest was rapid and ruthless; the torture, slow and bestial. The goal, in Heydrich's aseptic words, was "the housecleaning of Jews, intelligentsia, clergy, and the nobility."

One high army officer, General Johannes Blaskowitz, wrote a letter of complaint:

> *The unlimited brutalization and moral depravity . . . will spread like an epidemic through the most valuable German human material. If the high officials and SS continue to call for violence and brutality, brutal men will soon reign supreme. With disconcerting speed depraved birds of a feather find one another out and band together in order to satisfy their pathological and bestial instincts—as they are now doing in Poland. They can be barely kept in hand; for they have good reason to feel that they have official sanction to commit the most horrible of acts.*

But neither he nor the other German generals made any effective attempt to stop the atrocities. The High Command knew of Hitler's war plans before the war started, and they did their best to carry them out.

When Hitler broke his pact with Stalin and invaded Russia in June 1941, the frenzied killing was renewed. Five million Jews were living under the Soviet flag, four million of them in territories the Germans would overrun. About a million and a half of these fled or were evacuated before the Nazi troops arrived. The slaughter of those who remained was enormous. The mobile killing squads murdered 7,000 in Lvov, 2,500 in Zhitomir, 11,000 in Dnepropetrovsk, 15,000 in Rovno, 14,000 in Kharkov. . . . In Kiev, 35,000 Jews were marched to the Babi Yar ravine and shot. All in just two days, a tribute to German efficiency. A few months later, another 15,000 Jews were murdered in Kiev.

In the town of Zagrodski, in the Pinsk district, lived some 500 Jewish families. A killing squad arrived in mid-August 1942. The Jews were ordered to leave everything in their houses, take only their children, and come out to the square for a rollcall. Trucks rolled up, and the Jews were jammed aboard. There wasn't room for everyone, so the rest were ordered to run after the trucks. A young mother, Rivka Yosselevscka, was among them. After the war, she told a court what happened:

Q: And you ran with your daughter?
A: I had my daughter in my arms and ran after the truck. There were mothers who had two or three children and held them in their arms—running after the truck. We ran all the way. There were those who fell—we were not allowed to help them rise. They were shot—right there—wherever they fell. . . . When we reached the destination, the people from the truck were already down and they were undressed—all lined up. All my family was there. . . .
Q: Where was that?
A: This was some 3 kilometers from our village. . . . There was a kind of hillock. At the foot of this little hill, there was a dugout. We were ordered to stand at the top of the hillock and the four devils shot us—each one of us separately.
Q: Now these four—to what German unit did they belong?
A: They were SS men—the four of them. They were armed to the teeth. They were real messengers of the Devil and the Angel of Death.
Q: Please go on—what did you see?
A: When I came [to] the place—we saw people naked lined up. But we were still hoping that this was only torture. Maybe there is hope—hope of living. One could not leave the line, but I wished to see—what are they doing on the hillock? Is there anyone down below? I turned my head and saw that some three or four rows were already killed—on the ground. There were some twelve people amongst the dead. I also want to mention that my child said while we were lined up in the ghetto, she said, "Mother, why did you make me wear the Shabbat dress; we are being taken to be shot"; and when we stood near the dugout, near the grave, she said, "Mother, why are we waiting, let us run!" Some of the young people tried to run, but they were caught immediately, and they were shot right there. It was difficult to hold on to the children. We took all children not ours, and we carried—we were

anxious to get it all over—the suffering of the children was difficult; we all trudged along to come nearer to the place and to come nearer to the end of the torture of the children. The children were taking leave of their parents, and parents, of their elder people.

PRESIDING JUDGE: How did you survive through all this?

ATTORNEY-GENERAL: She will relate it.

PRESIDING JUDGE: Please will you direct the witness.

WITNESS: We were driven; we were already undressed; the clothes were removed and taken away; our father did not want to undress; he remained in his underwear. We were driven up to the grave, this shallow. . . .

ATTORNEY-GENERAL: And these garments were torn off his body, weren't they?

A: When it came to our turn, our father was beaten. We prayed, we begged with my father to undress, but he would not undress; he wanted to keep his underclothes. He did not want to stand naked.

Q: And then they tore them off?

A: Then they tore the clothing off the old man and he was shot. I saw it with my own eyes. And then they took my mother and shot her too; and then there was my grandmother, my father's mother, standing there; she was eighty years old and she had two children in her arms. And then there was my father's sister. She also had children in her arms and she was shot on the spot with the babies in her arms.

Q: And finally it was your turn.

A: And finally my turn came. There was my younger sister, and she wanted to leave; she prayed with the Germans; she asked to run, naked; she went up to the Germans with one of her friends; they were embracing each other; and she asked to be spared, standing there naked. He looked into her eyes and shot the two of them. They fell together in their embrace, the two young girls, my sister and her young friend. Then my second sister was shot and then my turn did come.

Q: Were you asked anything?

A: We turned towards the grave and then he turned around and asked, "Whom shall I shoot first?" We were already facing the grave. The Germans asked, "Who do you want me to shoot first?" I did not answer. I felt him take the child from my arms. The child cried out and was shot immediately. And then he aimed at me. First he held on to my hair and turned my head around; I stayed standing; I heard a shot, but I continued to stand and then he turned my head again and he aimed the revolver at me and ordered me to watch and then turned my head around and shot at me. Then I fell to the ground into the pit amongst the bodies, but I felt nothing. The moment I did feel, I felt a sort of heaviness and then I thought—maybe I am not alive anymore, but I feel something after I died. I thought I was dead, that this was the feeling which comes after death. Then I felt that I was choking; people falling over me. I tried to move and felt that I was alive and that I could rise. I was strangling. I heard the shots and I was praying for another bullet to put an end to my suffering, but I continued to move about. I felt that I was choking, strangling, but I tried to save myself, to find some air to breathe, and then I felt that I was climbing towards the top of the grave above the bodies. I rose, and I felt bodies pulling at me with their hands, biting at my legs, pulling me down, down. And yet with my last strength I came up on top of the grave, and when I did, I did not know the place, so many bodies were lying all over, dead people; I wanted to see the end of this stretch of dead bodies but I could not. It was impossible. They were lying, all dying; suffering; not all of them dead, but in their last sufferings; naked; shot, but not dead. Children crying "Mother," "Father"; I could not stand on my feet.

PRESIDING JUDGE: Were the Germans still around?

WITNESS: No, the Germans were gone. There was nobody there. No one standing up.

ATTORNEY-GENERAL: And you were undressed and covered with blood?

WITNESS: I was naked, covered with blood, dirty from the other bodies, with the excrement from other bodies, which was poured on me.

Q: What did you have in your head?

A: When I was shot, I was wounded in the head.

Q: Was it in the back of the head?

A: I have a scar to this day from the shot by the Germans; and yet, somehow I did come out of the grave. This was something I thought I would never live to recount. I was searching among the dead for my little girl, and I cried for her—Merkele was her name—"Merkele!" There were children crying "Mother!" "Father!"—but they were all smeared with blood and one could not recognize the children. I cried for my daughter. From afar I saw two women standing. I went up to them. They did not know me. I did not know them, and then I said who I was, and then they said, "So you survived." And there was another woman crying, "Pull me out from amongst the corpses, I am alive, help!" We were thinking how could we escape from the place. The cries of the woman, "Help, pull me out from the corpses!" We pulled her out. Her name was Mikla Rosenberg. We removed the corpses and the dying people who held on to her and continued to bite. She asked us to take her out, to free her, but we did not have the strength.

ATTORNEY-GENERAL: It is very difficult to relate, I am sure, it is difficult to listen to, but we must proceed. Please tell us now: after that you hid?

A: And thus we were there all night, fighting for our lives, listening to the cries and the screams, and all of a sudden we saw Germans, mounted Germans. We did not notice them coming in because of the screamings and the shoutings from the bodies around us.

Q: And then they rounded up the children and the others who had got out of the pit and shot them again?

A: The Germans ordered that all the corpses be heaped together into one big heap and with shovels they were heaped together, all the corpses, amongst them many still alive, children run-

69

ning about the place. I saw them. I saw the children. They were running after me, hanging on to me. Then I sat down in the field and remained sitting with the children around me. The children who got up from the heap of corpses.

Q: Then the Germans came again and rounded up the children?

A: Then Germans came and were going around the place. We were ordered to collect all the children, but they did not approach me, and I sat there watching how they collected the children. They gave a few shots and the children were dead. They did not need many shots. The children were almost dead, and this Rosenberg woman pleaded with the Germans to be spared, but they shot her.

ATTORNEY-GENERAL: Mrs. Yosselevscka, after they left the place, you went right next to the grave, didn't you?

A: They all left—the Germans and the non-Jews from around the place. They removed the machine guns and they took the trucks. I saw that they all left, and the four of us, we went onto the grave, praying to fall into the grave, even alive, envying those who were dead already and thinking what to do now. I was praying for death to come. I was praying for the grave to be opened and to swallow me alive. Blood was spurting from the grave in many places, like a well of water, and whenever I pass a spring now, I remember the blood which spurted from the ground, from that grave. I was digging with my fingernails, trying to join the dead in that grave. I dug with my fingernails, but the grave would not open. I did not have enough strength. I cried out to my mother, to my father, "Why did they not kill me? What was my sin? I have no one to go to." I saw them all being killed. Why was I spared? Why was I not killed?

And I remained there, stretched out on the grave, three days and three nights.

While the mobile killing units were at work in the Ukraine, a German civilian, serving as a construction engineer, happened to be on the scene when the ghetto in Dubno was wiped out. After the war, Hermann Graebe testified to what he had seen:

70

On October 5, 1942, when I visited the building office at Dubno, my foreman Hubert Moennikes told me that in the vicinity of the site, Jews from Dubno had been shot in three large pits, each about 30 meters long and 3 meters deep. About 1,500 persons had been killed daily. All of the 5,000 Jews who had been living in Dubno before the pogrom were to be liquidated. As the shootings had taken place in his presence, he was still much upset. . . .

Moennikes and I went directly to the pits. Nobody bothered us. Now I heard rifle shots in quick succession, from behind one of the earth mounds. The people who had got off the trucks— men, women and children of all ages—had to undress upon the order of an SS man who carried a riding or dog whip. They had to put down their clothes in fixed places, sorted according to shoes, top clothing, and underclothing. I saw a heap of shoes of about 800 to 1,000 pairs, great piles of underlinen and cloth- ing. Without screaming or weeping these people undressed, stood around in family groups, kissed each other, said farewells and waited for a sign from another SS man, who stood near the pit, also with a whip in his hand.

During the fifteen minutes that I stood near the pit, I heard no complaint or plea for mercy. I watched a family of about eight persons, a man and woman, both about fifty, with their children of about one, eight and ten, and two grown-up daughters of about twenty and twenty-four. An old woman with snow-white hair was holding the one-year-old child in her arms and singing to it and tickling it. The child was cooing with delight. The couple were looking on with tears in their eyes. The father was holding the hand of a boy about ten years old and speaking to him softly; the boy was fighting his tears. The father pointed toward the sky, stroked his head, and seemed to explain something to him. At that moment the SS man at the pit shouted something to his comrade. The latter counted off about twenty persons and instructed them to go behind the earth mound. Among them was the family which I have mentioned.

I well remember a girl, slim and with black hair, who, as she passed close to me, pointed to herself and said, "Twenty-

three!" I walked around the mound, and found myself confronted by a tremendous grave. People were closely wedged
together and lying on top of each other so that only their heads
were visible. Nearly all had blood running over their shoulders
from their heads. Some of the people shot were still moving.
Some were lifting their arms and turning their heads to show
that they were still alive. The pit was already two-thirds full.
I estimated that it already contained about a thousand people.

I looked for the man who did the shooting. He was an SS
man, who sat at the edge of the narrow end of the pit, his feet
dangling into the pit. He had a tommy gun on his knees and
he was smoking a cigarette. The people, completely naked,
went down some steps which were cut in the clay wall of the
pit and clambered over the heads of the people lying there, to
the place where the SS man directed them. They lay down
in front of the dead or injured people; some caressed those who
were still alive and spoke to them in a low voice. Then I heard
a series of shots.

I looked into the pit and saw that the bodies were twitching
or the heads lying already motionless on top of the bodies that
lay before them. Blood was running from their necks. I was
surprised that I was not ordered away, but I saw that there were
two or three postmen in uniform nearby. The next batch was
approaching already. They went down into the pit, lined themselves up against the previous victims and were shot.

When I walked back, around the mound, I noticed another
truckload of people which had just arrived. This time it included sick and infirm people. An old, very thin woman with
terribly thin legs was undressed by others who were already
naked, while two people held her up. The woman appeared to
be paralyzed. The naked people carried the woman around the
mound. I left with Moennikes and drove in my car back to
Dubno.

On the morning of the next day when I again visited the site,
I saw about thirty naked people lying near the pit—about
30 to 50 meters away from it. Some of them were still alive;
they looked straight in front of them with a fixed stare and

seemed to notice neither the chilliness of the morning nor the workers of my firm who stood around. A girl of about twenty spoke to me and asked me to give her clothes and help her escape. At that moment we heard a fast car approach and I noticed that it was an SS detail. I moved away to my site. Ten minutes later we heard shots from the vicinity of the pit. The Jews still alive had been ordered to throw the corpses into the pit—then they themselves had to lie down in this to be shot in the neck.

By the end of the winter of 1941–42, more than 90 percent of the Jews trapped by the Germans east of the Soviet border were dead. The extermination of men, women, and children did not disturb Hitler. "Nature is cruel," he said. "Therefore, we, too, may be cruel. If I don't mind sending the pick of the German people into the hell of war without regret for the shedding of valuable German blood, then I have naturally the right to destroy millions of men of inferior races who increase like vermin."

OUR TOWN IS BURNING (ES BRENT)
By Mordecai Gebirtig

Translated from the Yiddish by Joseph Leftwich

Our town is burning, brothers, burning,
Our poor little town is burning.
Angry winds are fanning higher
The leaping tongues of flame and fire,
The evil winds are roaring!
Our whole town burns!

(Refrain)
And you stand looking on with folded arms,
And shake your heads.
You stand looking on with folded arms
While the fire spreads!

Our town is burning, brothers, burning,
Our poor little town is burning.
Tongues of flame are leaping,
The fire through our town goes sweeping,
Through roofs and windows pouring.
All around us burns.   (Repeat refrain.)

Our town is burning, brothers, burning.
Any moment the fire may
Sweep the whole of our town away,
And leave only ashes, black and gray,
Like after a battle, where dead walls stand,
Broken and ruined in a desolate land.   (Repeat refrain.)

Our town is burning, brothers, burning.
All now depends on you.
Our only help is what you do.
You can still put out the fire
With your blood, if you desire.

Don't look on with folded arms,
And shake your heads.
Don't look on with folded arms
While the fire spreads!

ES BRENT

Blai - bn   zol   a   pus - ter   shliad   shvar-tze   pus - te   vent.
Lesht mit   ai - er   ei - gn   blut   ba - vaist   vos   ihr   kent.

Un   ihr   shteit   un   kukt   a - zoi   zich   mit   far - leig - te
Shteit   nit   bri - der   ot   a - zoi   zich   mit   far - leig - te

hent.   Un   ihr   shteit   un   kukt   a - zoi zich vie
hent.   Shteit   nit   bri - der   un   kukt   a - zoi zich vie

un - zer shte - tl   brent.
un - zer shte - tl   brent.

3 times

Es

Fine

8

Phantoms
in the Ghetto

Soon Heydrich, Goering, Himmler, and other Nazi leaders began referring to the "Final Solution of the Jewish Question" whenever they meant the extermination of the Jews. The innocent-sounding abstraction may have spared such sensitive souls the pain of thinking about what they really meant to do. More likely, they wanted to conceal from others their murderous intentions.

Early in the Polish campaign, Hitler, Himmler, and Heydrich decided that the next stage in the Final Solution was to concentrate the Jews in a small area. They meant not only the Polish Jews but all the Jews of Germany, Austria, Czechoslovakia, and whatever other countries the Nazis might take over. In the orders Heydrich sent to the officers of the *Einsatzgruppen* in September 1939, he said they must distinguish between the "final aim, whose attainment will take some time," and the "steps necessary for reaching it, which can be applied more or less at once."

The interior of occupied Poland was set aside as the place to concentrate Jews whom the killing squads had not reached. Instead of sending the killers to the victims, the victims were now to be brought to the killers.

The region chosen contained several cities—Warsaw, Cracow, Lodz, Lvov, Lublin, Radom—with large numbers of Jews. Warsaw alone now held half a million Jews, the largest Jewish population of any city in the world except New York. All Jewish

communities of less than 500 were herded into the nearest concentration city.

At the head of this administrative region, called the General
Government, Hitler placed Dr. Hans Frank. A Munich lawyer, he
had been convicted several times of embezzlement in the Weimar
days, and had murdered a lawyer who once prosecuted him. He
prided himself on his love of good books and music. At the end of
his first year in office, he told his co-workers in Poland, "I could
not eliminate all lice and Jews in only one year. But in the course
of time, and if you will help me, this end will be attained."

Once the Jews were concentrated, and the central machinery
was set up, the closing-in of the ghettos began. It was in April
1940 that the first ghetto was created, in Lodz. The steps taken
were gradual. Warsaw came next, in October; then Cracow in
March 1941; Lublin and Radom in April; and Lvov in December. By the end of 1941 the ghettoizing process was almost
complete.

The methods used were essentially the same everywhere. Never
was the ghetto meant to be permanent. As Friedrich Uebelhoer,
one Nazi chief working on the problem, put it: "The creation of
the ghetto is, of course, only a transition measure. I shall deter-
mine at what time and with what means the ghetto—and thereby
also the city of Lodz—will be cleansed of Jews. In the end, at any
rate, we must burn out this bubonic plague."

To carry out their instructions, the Nazis set up a Jewish Council (called a *Judenrat* in German) in each ghetto. Its functions
were typically dual and opposite: to take charge of survival—
health, welfare, supplies; and to take charge of destruction—registration, records, police. Some who served on them thought the
Councils would run the internal affairs of the ghetto in the prewar
tradition of Jewish self-government, and speak for the Jews before
the Nazi authorities controlling the ghetto. The Nazis, of course,
were offering this pretense of self-government as a device to get
the Jews to cooperate in their own extermination. It was a fiend-
ishly clever idea to put the blame for their degradation and destruction upon the Jews themselves. The intention was to

paralyze the Jews in the ghetto while they waited, consciously or unconsciously, for the Final Solution.

The ghettos were placed in the poorest part of each city. Jews who lived outside the ghetto areas were driven from their homes, robbed of their possessions, and jammed into cramped quarters with many other families. The Jews of surrounding towns were herded into the cities and thrown into the ghettos. Stone, brick, wood, and barbed wire sealed each ghetto off from the outside world. To be caught outside meant death.

In Czernowitz the Nazis mapped out a ghetto and ordered 50,000 Jews to move into it within eight hours. The mayor of the city, Traian Popovicz, recorded what happened:

> I looked out the window of my bedroom and amidst the flying flakes of the early snow I saw a scene which was incredible. In the streets was a vast crowd of wandering people. The aged were helped by children, there were women with infants in their arms, cripples dragging their lame frames. All had bundles in their hands or were pushing small carriages loaded with boxes. Some carried their burden on their backs: luggage, bundles of linen, cushions, blankets, clothing, rags. They were beginning their mute pilgrimage to their vale of tears, the Ghetto.
>
> Only one who knows the topography of Czernowitz can grasp how inadequate was the space reserved for the Ghetto. . . . This section that could hardly have accommodated 10,000 people had to house 50,000 Jews plus the Christian population which lived there. . . . Many were forced to live in corridors, cellars, garages, under bridges, anywhere to find shelter against snow and rain. Of the hygienic conditions I don't even speak. No sanitary water to drink . . . the pungent smell of sweat, urine, and excrement, of loathsome humidity . . . exactly like the smell of a flock of sheep in the field.

Lublin became the concentration point for Jews from western Poland, Bohemia, and Austria. Before the war the town held

72,000 Gentiles and 40,000 Jews. Now many times that number of Jews were penned into the ghetto. A journalist, S. Moldawer, described what he saw on the streets:

> Lublin is a vale of sorrow. No human beings are they who walk its streets; all are phantoms, shadows, haunting a world that is no longer in evidence. Nobody speaks in Lublin; nobody exchanges greetings. They have even ceased to weep. . . . The congestion, the stench, the poverty, the disease and the chaos which reign in Lublin cannot be paralleled anywhere on earth. Men live in the streets, in cattle stalls, in cellars, in carts and in the debris of devastated houses.
>
> Men die like flies in the thoroughfares, their bodies strewn on the roadway like old cinders. Shrouds are no longer used for the dead because none can be bought. . . . The whole city is girt with barbed wire fences, and the Nazis allow no traffic to pass through it. The water has turned foul and cannot be drunk. All the wells have become polluted. Cholera and typhus were already rampant when we reached Lublin. . . . The communal soup kitchen can actually serve nothing but potato broth and stale, black bread. Hundreds have not slept for weeks, cramped and confined in noisy freight cars. They wander about sad-eyed and distraught, like mourners at funerals. . . . One thing is as clear as the day: the devil himself could not have devised such hell. . . .

But even in the hell of such ghettos, people struggled to live the normal lives they once knew. Mark Dworzecki, a young physician of Vilna, continued to practice medicine there after the Nazis turned it into a huge prison for the Jews. From his diary of a day in the ghetto comes this entry, headed EIGHT P.M.:

> The young people are taking their evening stroll in twos and threes. The streets are very crowded.
>
> Youngsters laugh and joke, exchange glances, flirt, forgetting for the moment the grim squalor and the ever-present sense of dread that pervades the ghetto.

Thronged main streets. Rudnitzka, Shavelska, Strashun
Streets look almost festive. The ghetto café offers black, un-
sweetened coffee-roasted bran extract.

Romantic couples stroll to the yard of the Judenrat. There
stands a tree—the only tree in the ghetto—giving the illusion
of a park.

The lumberyard at 6 Strashun Street is the tryst for young
lovers. Perched on the heaps of timber they hold hands and
sing the sad, stirring Russian songs. Refrains are caught up,
voices blend:

> *We shall meet again*
> *At the cannon's breech . . .*

There is a performance at the ghetto theater. In the ghetto
café people crowd around the little tables, recounting the
hardships and horrors of the day. The evening prayers are
recited in the synagogue. Committees of the Underground hold
their consultations. The ghetto choirs sing Hebrew and Yiddish
songs.

News bulletins of the Partisan Organization circulate from
hand to hand.

Starving the Jews to death was cheaper than shooting them.
The Nazis looted the occupied countries of food and sent it to
Germany. They left barely enough to keep the Poles alive and less
for the ghetto Jews. Once the barbed wire went up, the Jews were
cut off from the open market. The Judenrat alone could buy and
distribute food. Theft, bribery, and favoritism had full play.
Under the grave shortages, black markets and smuggling sprang
up. Smugglers made it possible for some to survive a bit longer. If
they managed to retain something of value, they would swap it
for food. Jews who were allowed some liberty of movement out-
smarted the police and the SS who guarded the ghetto. Levi
Shalit observed how one woman, called Baylke, did it:

More than once Baylke has come face to face with death.
More than once bullets have grazed her as she leaps over the

barbed wire fence. But now that she has the task of transporting excrement out of the city, there is much less risk.

Actually her husband was assigned to the job, but Baylke, who is more capable and more daring, seizes the reins in her chunky hands and drives the horse herself. The cart filled with feces trundles on two huge wheels through all the remote streets of the town to the public toilets, which the city council has ordered to be cleaned. After they are emptied, the waste is deposited outside the city.

Baylke is everywhere, constantly in touch with her Christian neighbors in the surrounding villages; she sells them everything the ghetto gives her in exchange for produce. Her hiding place is safe—inside the sealed tin box in the cart of excrement.

Twice a day, at noon and in the evening, she rides into the ghetto, takes the hidden box from the wagon and removes from it bread, butter, fat and meat.

Everyone in the ghetto knows where Baylke takes the merchandise but nobody objects. On the contrary—they plead with her to take something to sell or exchange. They know their things won't get lost or confiscated. Not from Baylke's hiding place.

The two largest ghettos were in Warsaw and Lodz. In Warsaw, half a million Jews were forced within the walls. A third of the city's total population was sardined into 1.3 percent of the city's total area. Lodz had the most elaborate Judenrat imposed on its 160,000 Jews.

In some places, the Councils were made up of the men who had been the community leaders before the occupation. Or the local Nazi chief simply told the nearest rabbi to make up a Judenrat list on the spot. There were Jews who volunteered to serve, and others who were forced. If everyone refused to volunteer, as happened in one little town near Vilna, the community had to gather and draw lots for the Judenrat. The Councils consisted mostly of people with higher education or in the professions. There were few workers or artisans among them.

Whatever the method of selection, the Councils were caught

in the Nazi trap. At first, their functions embraced chiefly welfare: food rationing, job allocation, health and sanitation, housing, schooling, even policing. But then came the duty of providing forced-labor contingents for the Nazis. And as food supplies shrank and hunger increased, the Councils had to choose which categories of Jew should get food enough to stay alive (children? women? men? the old? the sick? the healthy? the rich? the poor?). Later, when the call came for what the Nazis deceptively called "resettlement" selection, the Councils were ordered to identify and register the victims, confiscate their posessions, and round them up for deportation to what, in fact, were death camps.

The Councils, their staffs, and their police forces became agents of the Nazi killing machine and instruments of their own execution. Can they be condemned outright and wholesale? Could they have done anything else but carry out the functions dictated by the Nazis? As with any manifestation of human behavior, the answer is not simple. Every Council member was a unique person, a complex of qualities: brave, cowardly, honest, corrupt, docile, aggressive, strong, weak, intelligent, stupid. And as a body, each Council performed in its own unique way. How estimate the role played by the Councils? Isaiah Trunk asks that question in the last chapter of his massive study of the Judenrat. And he says, "No historian of the catastrophe era can escape raising the question: Did the Councils in their strategy toward the Germans really exercise some justifiable policy that warranted, at least in their own minds, the hope of a delay or amelioration of the ominous end?" Trunk himself does not give a direct answer. But in his and many other studies there is ample evidence now of what the Councils did. Some followed the desperate principle of "Rescue Through Work." In Bialystok, Poland, the Council president was an engineer, Ephraim Barash. He tried to prove to the Nazis that the 50,000 Jews of his ghetto were so useful as workers that they were worthy of preservation. For a time Bialystok was treated as a peaceful "show ghetto." But inevitably the Nazis destroyed this ghetto, like all the others, and with the help of Barash's treachery. He ended up dishonored, an enemy of his people.

The Jewish police in the ghettos were patterned after the Nazi police. They wore black caps with blue Stars of David on them. Like the Nazi police, they had no justice department standing above to see that human and legal rights were being protected. No matter what an individual Jewish policeman might have desired to do, he could only be a tool of Nazi policy. The police themselves were the law, subject in this case, of course, to Nazi orders handed down through the Judenrat.

In Warsaw, the Judenrat recruited 2,000 men between the ages of thirty and thirty-five for the Jewish police force. Their commander was Sherinsky, a Jew converted to Christianity who had once been a Warsaw police captain. He had a notorious record as a Jew-hater, but it had not saved him from being locked into the ghetto with his "racial brothers." Later he was killed by the underground.

Ghetto life under the Nazis has been likened by some historians to Black slavery in the United States. One teacher and scholar who lived inside the Warsaw ghetto made the same analysis, except that he saw it as even worse in important respects. He was Emmanuel Ringelblum, who founded the Oneg Shabbat, the secret archives of the Warsaw ghetto. With the help of others, he collected documents and wrote his own notes on day-to-day events from January 1940 to early 1943. With his family, he was murdered by the Nazis, but his notes were found later in the ruins of the ghetto. This passage from them was headed "The Signs of Modern Slaves":

1. *Numbered and stamped.*
2. *Live in barracks—without their wives.*
3. *Wives and children removed, because slaves don't require families.*
4. *Walk in crowds, not individually.*
5. *Beaten and terrorized at work.*
6. *Inhuman exploitation . . .*
7. *Ban on organization of any kind.*
8. *Ban on any form of protest or sign of dissatisfaction.*
9. *Every slave dependent for his life on his master . . .*

84

10. The murderous discipline . . .
11. Compulsion to work . . .
12. Worse off than slaves, because they must look after their own food.
13. Confiscation of property from a dead worker's family, because the right of inheritance has been abolished.
14. Locked inside the residential block.
15. Ban on leaving your apartment and walking in the street after work hours.
16. Limitation of personal freedom, of movement.
17. Worse than slaves, because the latter knew they would remain alive, had some hope to be set free. The Jews are morituri—sentenced to death—whose death sentence [has been] postponed indefinitely, or has been passed.
18. The sick and the weak are not needed, so ambulatory clinics, hospitals and the like have been liquidated.

And the children in the ghettos? Ludwik Hirszfeld remembers those he watched in Warsaw:

The streets are so overpopulated, it is difficult to push one's way through. Everyone is ragged, in tatters. Often they no longer even possess a shirt. Everywhere there is noise and uproar. The thin piteous voices of children crying their wares—"Pretzels, cigarettes, sweets!"—are heard above the din.

No one will ever be able to forget those children's voices. . . .

There are always countless children inside the ghetto. People on the "Aryan" side gape curiously at the piteous spectacle presented by these tattered gangs. In fact, these gangs of children are the ghetto breadwinners. If the German looks away for one second, they run nimbly over to "Aryan" side. The bread, potatoes and other things that they buy are hidden under their rags, and then they have to slip back the way they came.

Not all the German sentries are murderers and executioners but unfortunately, many of them do not hesitate to take up their guns and fire at the children. Every day—it's almost unbelievable—children are taken to hospital with gunshot wounds.

The thousands of ragged beggars are reminiscent of a famine in India. Horrifying sights are to be seen every day. Here a half-starved mother is trying to suckle her baby at a breast that has no milk. Beside her may lie another, older child, dead. One sees people dying, lying with arms and legs outstretched, in the middle of the road. Their legs are bloated, often frostbitten, and their faces, distorted with pain. I hear that every day the beggar children's frostbitten fingers and toes, hands and feet are amputated.

I once asked a little girl: "What would you like to be?" "A dog," she answered, "because the sentries like dogs."

Yes, they treated dogs better than children. Here is what W. Szpilman saw in the ghetto one day, as he was walking along the inside wall:

I came across a smuggling operation being carried out by children. The actual operation seemed to be over. There was only one thing to do. The little Jewish boy on the other side of the wall had to slip back into the ghetto through the hole, bringing with him the last piece of booty. Half of the little boy was already visible, when he began to cry out. At the same time loud abuse in German could be heard from the "Aryan" side. I hurried to help the child, meaning to pull him quickly through the hole. Unhappily, the boy's hips stuck fast in the gap of the wall. Using both hands, I tried with all my might to pull him through. He continued to scream dreadfully. I could hear the police on the other side beating him savagely. When I finally succeeded in pulling the boy through the hole, he was already dying. His backbone was crushed.

It was only "natural," then, for the children to include death in the games they played. Dr. Aaron Peretz recalls what he saw in the Kovno ghetto:

The children in the ghetto would play and laugh, and in their games the entire tragedy was reflected. They would play grave digging: they would dig a pit and put a child inside and call him Hitler. And they would play at being gatekeepers of the ghetto. Some of the children played the parts of Germans; some, of Jews; and the Germans were angry and would beat the other children who were Jews. And they used to play funerals. . . .

The two-line rhymes of this ghetto song, expressing the Jews' courageous will to survive, were sung to a lilting Hasidic melody.

Vos darfn mir veynen, vos darfn mir klogn,
Mir veln noch frankn a kadish noch zogn.

Lomir zayn freylech un zogn zich vitsn,
Mir veln noch hitlern shive noch zitsn.

Lomir zich treystn, di tsores fargesn,
Es veln di verim noch hitlern fresn.

Di sonim, vos firn undz dort kayn treblinke,
Zey veln noch vern in der erd ayngezinken.

Mir veln tsuzamen noch orem bay orem,
Imirtseshem tantsn oyf daytshishe kvorim.

Why should we weep, why should we mourn,
We'll live to say the prayer of the dead for Frank.

Let us be gay and tell jokes,
We'll yet live to see Hitler dead.

Let us comfort one another and forget our troubles,
The worms will yet gnaw at Hitler.

The enemies who lead us there to Treblinka
Will yet be sinking into the earth.

Together we will yet, arm in arm,
With the help of God, dance on the graves of the Germans.

9

Gangs of Slaves

The Jews under German control were treated like a natural re-
source to be exploited until nothing was left. An official decree
began this treatment.

> *All Jews from fourteen to sixty years of age are subject to*
> *forced labor. . . . Jews called up for forced labor must report*
> *promptly and must bring food for two days and their bedding.*
> *Skilled Jewish workers must report with their tools. . . .*

Forced labor began at once, to clear away the rubble of war. At
first, when the Nazis needed labor, they would seize people off the
ghetto streets. In Warsaw, the Judenrat halted the terrifying press
gangs by organizing forced-labor squads and putting them at the
disposal of any Nazi agency which wanted them. The labor columns were paid little or nothing to do the emergency day-to-day
jobs. Gradually, when large-scale projects began and a more stable
kind of labor was required, the Nazis organized special concentration camps for specific use as slave-labor installations. At first, the
inmates were used on outdoor projects: to dig canals and anti-
tank ditches, to build roads and railways, to reclaim land or to
control floods. Then, industrial production was started up, and
factories erected near camps, or camps near factories. Jews were
used in aircraft plants, steel works, munitions factories, food
depots—everywhere the war effort required them.

The "useful" Jews were put up for sale by the SS at daily labor rates. The others—the weak, the sick, and the old—were classified as "unproductive" Jews. Their fate was a quicker death. The younger, healthier Jews went more slowly, worked into the grave, starved into the grave. Pay? On some military projects the army allowed about 40 cents a day. The other official agencies usually paid nothing for the forced labor they requisitioned. Food? So little that newcomers lost 50 pounds in weight in the first few months. Hours? Daybreak to nightfall, every single day of the week, all the year round.

Not only the Jews, of course, but civilians all over the conquered territories of Europe were conscripted for labor. They were corralled and herded into boxcars. Often without food, water, or sanitary facilities, they were shipped to Germany. They worked in factories, fields, and mines, and were beaten and starved and often left to die for lack of food, clothing, and shelter. By late 1944 there were 7½ million such civilians, plus another 2 million prisoners of war, grinding out their lives for Hitler's Germany.

The system of forced labor provided the majority of German firms—Krupp, I. G. Farben, Hermann Goering, Siemens, Roechling, etc.—with gangs of slaves. No law protected the worker. The Red Cross was not allowed to intervene.

The industrialists, suffering from a manpower shortage, besieged the SS with applications for slave labor, arguing that only thus could they carry out their "patriotic duty" to the war effort. The businessmen and the SS got along beautifully. The firms profited by the miserable wages they paid directly to the camps that farmed out the workers. (The prisoners never saw one cent of their earnings.) And the SS, collectively and through personal graft, profited by the deals made with the companies.

Living conditions in the camps were wretched, and if disease did not finish them off first, the inmates were marked "unfit for labor" and sent off to a worse fate. The idea was to kill through labor. Of the 35,000 Jews who worked making synthetic rubber for the I. G. Farben *Bunawerk* (Buna plant) at Auschwitz, at least 25,000 died. Their life expectancy was three or four months. In the coal mines it was one month. But it did not bother the corporation executives. Every day there was a fresh delivery of slaves.

The labor camps soon spread over the conquered territories like a giant spiderweb. Most were built close to large towns, within easy reach of railways. Everywhere in the labor camps, Himmler had the SS post signs for the enlightenment of the prisoners. They read:

THERE IS A ROAD TO FREEDOM. ITS MILESTONES ARE:
OBEDIENCE, HARD WORK, HONESTY, SOBRIETY, CLEANLINESS,
DEVOTION, ORDER, DISCIPLINE AND PATRIOTISM.

The prisoners soon knew better. What road to freedom was marked by hunger, cold, filth, and torture?

Reuben Rosenberg, eleven years old when the war began, lived in Lublin. The Nazis seized him for forced labor. They sent him to one camp after another. He tells of his experiences, beginning at Deblin:

> I worked at the aviation depot for the Werman firm, later owned by Schultz. The work was difficult, canalization, concrete and other tasks. Sometimes youngsters deliberately wounded their feet on the rails to be freed of the labor for a few days. The work was unbearable. Two boys were killed for stealing potatoes. They were dragged to the cellar of the gendarmerie, where dogs bit them to death. . . .

Then he was sent to Czestochowa:

> There were two work places here, the iron foundry, Rakov, and Felzer, an ammunition factory. The food was bad, the labor hard, and we were almost naked. They divided up those from Deblin. There were 700 of us. The three barracks were surrounded by barbed wire. Two people slept on one straw sack; there were 250 men, infested with vermin, sleeping in each barrack. . . . We worked in the iron foundry in two shifts, three shifts in transportation. . . . At Rakov the work—loading

iron, tar, coal and coke—was very hard. There were some terrible accidents at the workshops. Men fell asleep from hunger or fatigue at their machines, and their hands or feet would be torn away. . . .

For work we had to rise at 4 A.M., walk 2 kilometers to the station and detour 10 kilometers to Weimar. We worked from nine to four, with frequent rollcalls. There was one loaf of bread and some soup for five people. Twice a week there was sausage. Our work was to clean up the debris after a bombing; there were air attacks every day. We dragged German corpses from the cellars. . . .

Later he moved to Flossenbürg:

At this camp there was a factory that made bazookas. There was one SS man for every four prisoners. Every day 15 men died, aside from those who died from "natural causes." We ran to work. Work intended for 20 people was done by 10. We worked from 6 A.M. to 7 P.M. We collapsed. Many people committed suicide. In two weeks 500 died. Filth, no water, two days without heat, no bath, and no underwear. There was twenty-five lashes for stealing potato peelings. They called us the race gang, communists, cadets, soapbags, criminals, and bolsheviks. . . .

Because things were bad at the front, they hurried us and always beat us at the factory. . . . To load bazookas we had to use picric acid and trotil. We worked without gas masks, and after a few weeks the lungs and feet would cave in. The young were chosen for this task. SS men would kill them while they worked, so there was always a shortage of workers. . . .

One of the workers at Monowitz (the slave-labor camp attached to Auschwitz), which was built for the I. G. Farben Bunawerk, was Kai Feinberg. After the war, he told what slave labor did to his own family:

The conditions were intolerable. . . . On our first day of work, Christmas Eve, 24 December 1942, we had to work

through without food until 3 o'clock in the morning of 25
December. Our work consisted of unloading wagons of iron
bars and sacks of cement and heavy ovens. . . .

On 5 January 1943 my father was so weakened that he
collapsed before my eyes while having to haul along such a
50-kilo sack of cement at a running pace. I wanted to help him
but was hit and beaten back by an SS man with a stick. . . .

One of my father's brothers injured himself in the arm while
at work and was gassed. My father's second brother died from
weakness while at work in Buna one or two weeks after the
death of my father.

I myself withstood the work until 15 January 1943; then I
got pneumonia and worked again from 15 February until the
end of February. Then I was declared unfit for work because I
could no longer walk, and was due to be gassed. As it happened
no lorry going to the gas chambers came to the Bunawerk that
day and I was therefore taken back to the Auschwitz concentration camp.

A young German Jew, Hans Baermann of Cologne, was fourteen when the Nazis forced him out of school. With his parents
he was shipped east in December 1941, to the Riga ghetto in
Latvia. Two days after their arrival, Hans was among 200 young
Jews chosen for forced labor at the nearby Salaspils camp. This is
his account of what happened then:

Frozen and starved, we reached a snow-covered clearing that
held but a single, large, roofless barracks of wood. Some 4,000
Jews from southern Germany already lived in it, and they
attacked us like wolves for food and drink. Our hair was shorn
and we were then assigned, three men to a bunk 18 inches high,
6 feet long and less than 5 feet wide. It was bitter cold and the
slats were covered with ice. On the third day after our arrival
we saw our first bread and a horse-drawn sleigh loaded with
potato peelings from the SS kitchen at Riga.

An SS sergeant named Nickel introduced himself as the

Commandant, and immediately assigned us to work, to be performed without overcoats and without fires. The construction program embraced 45 barracks in which Latvians and Russians were later quartered. This program was fulfilled, all but 5 barracks. Watchtowers also had to be constructed and the entire area enclosed with barbed wire.

I spent seven months starving in this death camp. In the end I weighed only 80 pounds and was infected with lice. Reduced virtually to a skeleton, I was photographed for the Stürmer [Streicher's anti-Semitic magazine]. Of 15,000 men who passed through this camp, in time, virtually all wasted away. Only 192 survived. I was among them. . . .

The ghettos themselves were integrated as productive units into the German war machine. Inside the Warsaw ghetto, for example, factories operated by German industrialists put tens of thousands of Jews to work making clothing, textiles, brushes, shoes, mattresses, furniture, and barrack doors, windows, and roof sections. Most of the production was intended for the military, but the Germans bribed SS and army officials to divert some of it into private hands. The starved workers got a few zlotys and a sip of soup for twelve hours' work a day.

It was a tragically ironic situation. The German firms had a vested interest in hanging onto profitable ghetto laborers, and so, opposed killing them. And the Jewish workers clung to their jobs, helping the enemy with their own hands, for fear of being sent to the even worse labor camps, and later, the death camps. "The history of man," said Ringelblum, the Warsaw-ghetto archivist, "knows no similar tragedy. A nation that hates the Germans with all its soul can ransom itself from death only at the price of its contribution to the enemy's victory, a victory which means its complete extermination in Europe and perhaps in the whole world."

By the middle of 1944 the Jewish labor force was almost totally destroyed. Valuable as its work was for military needs, that purpose took second place in Hitler's mind to the goal of annihilation.

The exploitation of Jewish workers was merely a preliminary to their execution. Perhaps half a million Jews were killed off at forced labor or died of starvation and disease in the ghettos.

This is a song of the forced laborers whose endless hours of work on starvation rations brought huge numbers to early death.

Zuntog un Montog—ligt men in di griber,
Dinstog un Mitvoch—hot men fiber.
Donershtog un Fraytog—hakt men shteyner,
Shabes hot men tsubrochene beyner.

Shlofn shlofn men in di palatkes,
Nishto kayn hoyzn, nishto kayn gatkes,
Nishto kayn shich, nishto kayn shtivl,
Nishto kayn groshn tsu shraybn a brivl.

Sunday and Monday—we lie in the ditches,
Tuesday and Wednesday—we have the fever.
Thursday and Friday—we break stones,
On the Sabbath, we have aching bones.

We sleep in tents,
We have no pants nor underwear,
We have no shoes, we have no boots,
We haven't a penny to send a letter.

10

One Little Spark

When news of the forced-labor decree reached the Warsaw ghetto in January 1940, Chaim Kaplan wrote in his diary, "The Jews do not believe that it will come to pass."

Kaplan was principal of a pioneering elementary Hebrew school in Warsaw and the author of books for children on Jewish history. Like Emmanuel Ringelblum, he kept a secret diary. (The small notebooks were smuggled out of the ghetto; Kaplan and his wife are believed to have died in the Treblinka extermination camp.)

Two weeks later, again he was writing:

> From the outset the People of Hope did not believe that the decree of forced labor for the Jews would be put into effect. As is the way with Jews, they didn't understand the decree in its simple sense. Because of the magnitude of the destruction contained therein, they didn't believe that even so fierce an enemy as the Fuehrer would put it into actual practice. They tried to find in it some hint for an enormous financial contribution instead. . . .

In another two weeks, he was explaining why the Jews felt this way:

There is no room in our inner feelings for despair and depression. We greet every edict with a deprecating smile, although we are conscious that the creators and enactors of these cruel decrees are psychopaths. . . . A poison of hatred permeates the blood of the Nazis, and therefore all their stupid decrees, the fruit of this hatred, are doomed to failure. Such an awareness saves us from despair. Anything founded upon insanity must not last long.

By the end of May, Hitler's armies had subdued Western Europe. Yet, wrote Kaplan:

Our Jews don't believe in the murderer's victories in France. The newspapers announce victories which cannot be denied, whose truth is apparent—yet the Jews don't admit them. They stick to their conviction: The Germans will end in destruction. They got this far in the years 1914–1918, but nevertheless they were defeated in the end. Knowledgeable people are in mourning, but the masses are happy. They have entered Antwerp? Don't believe them! They conquered Rotterdam? Tell it to Grandma. The people's desire doesn't allow them even to consider the possibility that the murderers will win. The entire world will rise up against them. . . . This is the power of desire. It is the father of all thought.

Later, when mass deportations to mysterious "resettlement" places were sweeping out the ghettos, the same disbelief in reality gripped many. Oscar Pinkas, who lived through it, recalls the mood:

We watched and listened but did not know what it all meant. The normal process of thinking and reacting, the horror of the truth, and the deliberate confusion planted by the Germans, all these combined to produce a frightful weariness, a wish to get it over with—whatever that entailed: deportation, resettlement, concentration camp. . . . When we heard the rushing trains, we cried instinctively, "Heavens, we are all perishing."

96

But then, once assumed, that knowledge became impossible
to accept. We then went back to our daily routines. . . .

The "deliberate confusion" was a product of Nazi cunning.
The terror and violence, the contradictory commands, the lies,
the isolation from the outside world, the hunger, the playing off
of one section of Jewry against another—it was psychological
warfare designed to scatter reason and paralyze the will.

How does the mind of the victim work under such conditions
of stress? In May 1942 the Nazis began to visit Jews in their
Warsaw-ghetto apartments at night, and murder them. By shooting, clubbing, throwing them out of the windows. The people
could find no pattern in the isolated murders. None of the victims
knew each other or had anything in common, socially or economically. Then why *these* victims? Kaplan speculates in his diary:

> *In order to comfort ourselves, we feel compelled to find some*
> *sort of system to explain these nighttime murders. Everyone,*
> *afraid for his own skin, thinks to himself: If there is a system,*
> *every murder must have a cause; if there is a cause, nothing*
> *will happen to me since I am absolutely guiltless.*
>
> *But . . . the system is a lack of system. The guiding*
> *principle is the annihilation of a specific number of Jews every*
> *night. They go to the files, indiscriminately draw out a card, and*
> *whoever is picked, is picked; he is destined to die. . . .*
>
> *People do not want to die without cause.*

Bernard Goldstein said it in somewhat different words: "The
will to live was so strong that it created the illusions necessary to
sustain it."

Some of the Jews of Germany and Austria, who had found no
salvation through conversion, found it in death. With each new
Nazi decree, many killed themselves. But "not so with the beaten
down, shamed, broken Jews of Poland," said Kaplan.

> *They love life, and they do not wish to disappear from the*
> *earth before their time. This fact, that we have hardly any*

suicides, is worthy of emphasis. Say what you wish, this will of ours to live in the midst of terrible calamity is the outward manifestation of a certain hidden power whose quality has not yet been examined. It is a wondrous, superlative power with which only the most established communities among our people have been blessed.

We are left naked, but as long as this secret power is still within us, we do not give up hope. And the strength of this power lies in the indigenous nature of Polish Jewry, which is rooted in our eternal tradition that commands us to live. Polish Jewry says, together with our poet laureate Bialik:

> One spark is hidden in the stronghold of my heart
> One little spark, but it is all mine;
> I borrowed it from no one, nor did I steal it
> For it is of me, and within me.

Even during the deportation of over 300,000 Warsaw-ghetto Jews to the Treblinka death camp, there were relatively few suicides, Emmanuel Ringelblum noted.

> The large masses of the people, as well as the overwhelming majority of the intelligentsia, did not permit themselves to break down, and resisted passively as long as it was possible. As for the question why did the Jews not defend themselves? The answer is: They offered a strong and effective psychic resistance. No other people in the world could have endured psychically as long as the Jews.

One expression of that endurance was the cultural life that went on in the ghetto despite all the surrounding horror. Plays and concerts were allowed by the Germans so long as the dramatists and composers were not Aryan and the censor was not offended. But the Jews in the Warsaw ghetto got around the restrictions, said the Yiddish actor Jonas Turkow, and satire mocking the enemy was often performed. Five ghetto theaters produced plays, in Yiddish or Polish. There were both professional and amateur choruses and orchestras. About 1,800 performances were given in the year 1940–41.

In the Lodz ghetto, too, there was the same spontaneous creation of theatricals, concerts, lectures, classes, and reading circles. Writers wrote, actors acted, musicians played, incredible as it seems to us who never knew that life in death. What was created vanished in the destruction, except for a few things. Among them are these verses by the poet S. Shayevich:

> The Lord has showered even us with gentle hand:
>> A double gift—
> The death-decree and spring.
>> The garden blooms, and the sun shines.
>> And the slaughterer slaughters. . . .
> But we crave no recompense or mercy.
>> For when you slay a man
>> You slay his God as well.

Although the ghetto population was constantly changing, through death or deportation, schooling continued. Courses for adults were given in watchmaking, leatherwork, engraving, and drawing. Schools for Jewish children were closed under the pretext of epidemics, but secret or camouflaged schools were set up. The communal kitchens became one excuse for bringing children together in groups. Beneath their jackets they smuggled in the scarce texts and notebooks. N. Korn, the teacher of an underground school in Lublin, recalled the danger in his memoirs:

> With beating hearts we conducted the lessons, simultaneously on the alert for the barking voices of the SS, who frequently raided Jewish homes. In such a case all incriminating traces immediately disappeared. Gone were books and notebooks. The pupils began to play and the teacher became a customer: in a tailor's house he began to try on clothes and in a shoemaker's house—shoes.

On the site of a bombed-out house in the Warsaw ghetto, Jewish workers built swings and benches while the students of a graphic-arts workshop painted a fresco of playful animals on a ruined wall. The teachers went on teaching; they wanted the children to believe in a future. In a Jewish paper issued in the Cracow ghetto, a little girl named Martha published this poem:

> *I must be saving these days*
> *(I have no money to save),*
> *I must save health and strength,*
> *Enough to last me for a long while.*
> *I must save my nerves,*
> *And my thoughts, and my mind,*
> *And the fire of my spirit;*
> *I must be saving of tears that flow—*
> *I shall need them for a long, long while.*
> *I must save endurance these stormy days.*
>
> *There is so much I need in my life:*
> *Warmth of feeling and a kind heart—*
> *These things I lack; of these I must be saving!*
> *All these, the gifts of God,*
> *I wish to keep.*
> *How sad I should be*
> *If I lost them quickly.*

"Even more than bread," said the ghetto poet Leon Staf, "we now need poetry in a time when it seems that it is not needed at all."

As the Nazis began to rob Poland of its cultural treasures, shipping them off to Germany, the Jews worried about the fate of their own libraries. To save a major Jewish collection which had been closed and sealed off by the Nazis, Warsaw Bundists tunneled secretly under the walls and into the building. It took a week to carry out the more important volumes, hiding them under potatoes and coal. Then they set up small mobile libraries for both children and adults, operating secretly out of ghetto homes.

One of the first moves of the Germans had been to close all synagogues, houses of prayer, and ritual baths. They ordered that the Jews be made to work on the Sabbath and even on the High Holidays. But throughout Poland, the High Holidays were celebrated no matter what the Nazis decreed. For Hanukkah of 1940, the blinds in the Warsaw ghetto were drawn in rooms which faced the street, and in nearly every ghetto courtyard the feeling of national kinship was renewed.

At Sukkoth that year, the holiday was celebrated everywhere in the Warsaw ghetto, with the prayer groups saying the wine blessing. A large group of Hasidim (followers of the religious movement founded by Israel Baal Shem Tov) even danced outdoors, on Mila Street, singing the holiday songs in chorus, followed by a large crowd. "When they sang," wrote Kaplan, "they reached such a state of ecstasy that they couldn't stop until some heretic approached them, shouting, 'Jews! Safeguarding your life is a positive Biblical commandment; it is a time of danger for us. Stop this!' Only then did they become quiet. Some of them replied in their ecstasy, 'We are not afraid of the murderer! The devil with him!' "

By 1941 public worship and celebration was forbidden. Nevertheless, Purim of this Jewish year, 5701, was marked in the Warsaw ghetto. At the Zionist soup kitchen on 13 Zamenhof Street, said Chaim Kaplan, they read the Scroll, sang the holiday songs, and even had a bite to eat between numbers—bread and butter, a taste of the traditional poppy-seed tart, and a glass of sweetened coffee. "We came sad and left sad," he wrote, "but we had some pleasant moments in between. . . ."

One of the most moving achievements of the ghetto's underground was the creation and preservation of the Ringelblum Archives. Without them, we would know infinitely less about life in the Jewish communities of occupied Poland. Ringelblum had worked his way through the University of Warsaw, earning his doctorate in the history of Warsaw's Jews. He taught in a Warsaw high school and organized classes for adults throughout Poland. When the war broke out, he was thirty-nine, and in Geneva as a delegate to the World Zionist Congress. (He was a member of the Left-Poale Zionist group.) He could have remained abroad in safety, but he chose to go back to Poland. There he worked in the JDC's Warsaw office.

In the ghetto he gathered around him a secret organization to plan and carry out sociological studies of every aspect of ghetto life under the occupation. There were dozens of trained researchers in the group, teenagers among them. "Our aim was to present the whole truth, no matter how harsh it might be," he said. Papers were presented at secret Saturday meetings (hence the group's name, Oneg Shabbat—the pleasures of the Sabbath) and were discussed and reworked. By many clandestine means the group also gathered documents of both the Germans and the Judenrat, copies of the underground press, leaflets, diaries, poems, photos, all to build a collective portrait of Polish Jewry in World War II. "Death was the constant companion of its workers," said Hirsh Wasser, the secretary of Oneg Shabbat. "Day and night every member was threatened with the greatest danger, of which death was the most comfortable."

Ringelblum also headed the Warsaw ghetto's underground propaganda department and edited its illegal paper, News. In August 1942, when the mass deportations began, the archives and his own journal were buried in the ghetto. Two parts were discovered, in 1946 and 1950; the third part is still missing.

TEREZIN

The heaviest wheel rolls across our foreheads
To bury itself deep somewhere inside our memories.

We've suffered here more than enough,
Here in this clot of grief and shame,
Wanting a badge of blindness
To be a proof for their own children.

A fourth year of waiting, like standing above a swamp
From which any moment might gush forth a spring.

Meanwhile, the rivers flow another way,
Another way,
Not letting you die, not letting you live.

And the cannons don't scream and the guns don't bark
And you don't see blood here.

Nothing, only silent hunger.
Children steal the bread here and ask and ask and ask
And all would wish to sleep, keep silent and
    just to go to sleep again. . . .

The heaviest wheel rolls across our foreheads
To bury itself deep somewhere inside our memories.

(Mif, a child in the Terezin ghetto, 1944)

11

The Final Solution

It is early in February 1942 that rumors of a Nazi decision to exterminate the Jews reach the Warsaw ghetto. Chaim Kaplan notes in his diary a report that the Fuehrer "has decided to rid Europe of a whole people by simply having them shot to death." The same day he mentions that the Judenrat is planning a rollcall of ghetto Jews. People say that deportations begin with such a rollcall.

(Much earlier, in March 1940, it had been whispered to Kaplan that hundreds of young Jewish professionals who had been taken out of the ghetto had been deported to a camp called Auschwitz. But he knew little about that place or what happened to the prisoners there.)

At the end of February 1942 he hears that thousands of Jews have been killed somewhere "by poison gas." But he is sorrowing here and now over the deaths by starvation, in one week, of both his wife's sister and her husband. This is a commonplace in the ghetto, where at every turn one sees living skeletons.

On April 7, Kaplan trembles at the mention of Lublin. There an entire community of 44,000 Jews, he hears, is being wiped off the face of the earth. Panic-stricken Jews are being hunted down by the Nazis and taken "to some unknown place to be massacred." He asks himself, "Why should Warsaw fare better than Lublin?"

On April 12, Ringelblum records rumors that a German extermination brigade has arrived in Warsaw.

The rumors were true. Extermination of the Jews by gas had already begun in Poland. The whirlwind of death had not yet reached Warsaw, only because the gassing installation at Treblinka was not yet complete.

It was no secret in high Nazi circles that Hitler wanted to get rid of all the Jews. He had always said that this was his intention. It was there on the pages of *Mein Kampf*. And it had been repeated time and again in speeches and the press. Again the question: Then why didn't the Jews and others believe what he said?

For one thing, because no sane person took the threats to mean organized mass murder. The Nazis talked of forced emigration, yes, and even put forth a wild plan to convert the island of Madagascar into a concentration camp for all of Europe's Jews. Not until early 1939 did Hitler say publicly that if a war came, it would end in the annihilation of the Jews. But no evidence has come to light that the Nazis had prepared a plan for extermination. Only toward the end of 1940 did secret discussions of such a Final Solution begin.

Still, the groundwork for mass murder had been laid. The Jews had been humiliated and terrorized for years. Couldn't the next, and final, step be foreseen? Some few did predict it, but most people couldn't believe it would happen. Partly because we often screen out of our consciousness what we don't want to hear or can't bear to believe. But perhaps more because there is often a big gap between the declaration of an intention and the act of carrying it out. Who knew—*then*—whether Hitler really meant to replace the centuries-old policy of expulsion with annihilation? Or whether he would have the opportunity to go that far?

He had started slowly, waiting until his power was total, testing world opinion. And the other nations had done little to oppose or prevent the atrocities the Nazis had committed against the Jews for years. With the war, Hitler saw his chance to carry out the destruction of the Jews. Behind the battle lines he could keep secret the terrible "Final Solution of the Jewish Question."

It had begun in Poland with the mobile killing units and the starving of the ghetto inhabitants. But hunger took its toll too slowly. Some said it would need five years, others, eight years, to finish off the Jews that way. Hitler decided to use faster means.

On July 31, 1941, Goering sent Heydrich orders to make all necessary preparations "for a complete solution of the Jewish question in the German sphere of influence in Europe." Heydrich knew what the cryptic letter meant. He now had full authority to proceed with the killings. He had been preparing for them with the concentration of the Jews in the ghettos. He summoned Eichmann (his expert in Jewish affairs), told him "The Fuehrer has ordered the physical extermination of the Jews," and instructed him to organize the deportations to the death camps.

Eichmann arrived at Maidanek, the death camp near Lublin. "A German police captain there showed me how they managed to build airtight chambers disguised as ordinary Polish farmers' huts, seal them hermetically, then inject the exhaust gas from a Russian U-boat motor." Eichmann passed on Heydrich's order to start "liquidating a quarter million Polish Jews."

Then he went to Lodz, to see how Jews were being gassed. He watched a thousand of them packed into buses with closed windows. Carbon monoxide from the exhausts was piped back into the buses. The buses were driven to pits, the doors opened, and the corpses shoveled out. A Pole with a pair of pliers leaped into the pits, pried open the mouths, and tore out the gold teeth.

Asked to watch the execution through a peephole in a driver's seat, Eichmann declined because, he said, he "simply couldn't look at any suffering." He did observe, however, that the procedure was too slow. Within a few months German technical ingenuity speeded up the process. It could make anything more efficient, even the machinery of death.

After experiments at the Auschwitz concentration camp, whose construction had begun in January 1940, the first permanent death camp was completed at Chelmno. Everything looked ready now. Hans Frank met with his staff to remind them that if the Jews survived the war, victory would be in vain. "Gentlemen," he said, "I must ask you to arm yourselves against all feelings of sympathy. We have to annihilate the Jews wherever we find them and wherever it is at all possible."

The next step was to enlist the active help of all the agencies of the German government. To carry out the Final Solution swiftly and efficiently, the whole State apparatus was needed. The chiefs of these agencies were by now specially picked Nazis. But many of the career men in the civil service, the backbone of the operations, were trained pre-Hitler; many were not even in the Party. Heydrich anticipated great difficulty in getting their cooperation for the extermination.

He was wrong.

He learned how wrong when he called a conference of top ministry officials and SS generals at Wannsee, a Berlin suburb, on January 20, 1942. The aim was to coordinate the material and technical means required for the extermination of the 11 million Jews in occupied countries throughout Europe. The meeting lasted no more than ninety minutes, and was followed by drinks and lunch. Not only did no one object to the plans for the Final Solution, but with "boundless enthusiasm" useful proposals were made for improving upon the extermination process, which was already under way. The bureaucrats competed with each other for the honor of being foremost in this murderous matter.

Eichmann, who was the lowest-ranking official present, said he came away feeling "free of all guilt." If no one, no one at all, among these august personages, was against the Final Solution, then who was he to be troubled?

From the most respectable anti-Semite to the concentration-camp killer, the chain was solid. The Jew-baiter of any kind, as the Final Solution attests, is implicated in the criminal madness of a Hitler. Step by step the "mere" anti-Semite can be drawn into mass murder.

Within a few months of the Wannsee Conference, all the killing centers were ready. In addition to Chelmno, there was Treblinka, for Jews from the Warsaw and Bialystok districts. Sobibor, Belzec, and Maidanek, all in the Lublin district, would take deportees not only from there but from Cracow, Radom, Galicia, Czechoslovakia, and Holland. Auschwitz, located in

Upper Silesia, took Jews from many places, including all the conquered countries.

Trainloads of Jews from all over Europe began to stream into the six killing centers. The movement would not end until the German armies were crushed.

The deportations began in the winter of 1941–42. Even before the killing centers were ready, the Germans started to move the Jews closer to them. The Germans, of course, did not announce their true purpose. They said they intended simply to "resettle" Jews in the East. The "settlers" starved and froze in the temporary quarters. The German Jews were among the first to be "shipped East to work," for the Nazis were eager to rid the Third Reich of the last Jew. Some went to Lodz, others to Riga and Minsk, where they filled up the emptied Russian ghettos.

Jeanette Wolf of Berlin described her transport to Riga in January:

> We rode five days in the cold train without warm food and tortured by thirst. A few people at a time were permitted to leave each car to get water; and a few minutes were allowed for cleaning ourselves in the snow. Men and women had to perform their toilet on the rail embankment in each other's presence. In the terrible cold, hundreds of people froze parts of their bodies and developed gangrenous fingers and toes, and many died after reaching the camp. . . .
>
> At the Shirotava station in Riga, German and Latvian SS welcomed us with sticks and rifle butts. . . . The SS drove us to the ghetto. The houses looked as if vandals had visited them. Floors and stairs were littered with broken furniture and china, torn clothing and shoes, plaster and damaged household articles. Toilets and pipes had been smashed. It was obvious that the previous residents had left in great haste just before we came, but we did not at once understand why. We soon heard rumors that they had been killed. . . .
>
> During the first two weeks we received no food. We looked in the garbage for frozen potato peelings, vegetable refuse, and cleaned, cooked and ate the stuff. We mixed potato peelings

with flour and baked them without fat. The stoves were broken and smoked heavily. If an army bread truck driving through the ghetto stopped long enough, we stole bread. When food came, it was a starvation ration. . . . Friends who had come with us died of hunger and exposure. Most people had lost their will to live.

The deportees—all but a few, such as Jeanette Wolf—were annihilated, by shooting squads or by gas.

On July 22, mass deportation from the Warsaw ghetto began. Every day a train packed with at least 5,000 Jews would run the 60 miles from Warsaw to Treblinka. Within two months, 300,000 Jews were sent to their deaths. The Judenrat was given the task of delivering 6,000 Jews a day to the *Umschlagplatz,* a large yard behind a hospital, surrounded by a high brick wall. The Council announced exempt categories: Jews with work certificates; Jews fit for work, and their families; members of the Judenrat, its police and all its many other agencies, together with their families. The list was so long, it made many believe the worst had not yet come. It paralyzed the will to resist or to hide. This was "only" the "resettlement" of the weak and unproductive, people said; it was not the end.

The day after the deportations began, delegates of all Jewish groups met secretly to consider a course of action for the ghetto. Bernard Goldstein, a leader of the underground Bund, tells what his people thought:

All of us felt that active resistance and obstruction of the deportations was the only possible course. The ghetto had no right to sacrifice 60,000 human beings so that the survivors might continue their slave existence a little longer. Whether we could obtain weapons or not, we owed it to ourselves to resist, with bare hands if necessary. We could do at least some damage to the Germans by setting fire to the factories and warehouses inside the ghetto. Would it not be better to die in the flames than to wait our inevitable turn to follow the unfortunate 60,000?

But except for two left-wing Zionist groups, no one else at the meeting supported the Bund's position. They gave way to panic, clinging to the illusions of the majority in the ghetto. In its illegal bulletin, *Storm*, the Bund called on the 60,000 not to report voluntarily for death but to go into hiding, to resist, to fight to the end.

Day after day Chaim Kaplan watched the expulsions from the ghetto.

> *The ghetto has turned into an inferno. Men have become beasts. Everyone is but a step away from deportation; people are being hunted down in the streets like animals in the forest. It is the Jewish police who are cruelest toward the condemned.*

The police ringed a house or a whole block at a time, and went from door to door demanding documents. Whoever had neither the right document nor money enough for bribes was told to gather up a bundle and board the truck at the gate. People were seized on the streets, too, and taken to the *Umschlagplatz* as they were, with no good-byes. It was horrible, says Bernard Goldstein.

> *Children hung onto their fathers, wives to their husbands. They grabbed at pieces of furniture, doorjambs, anything to keep from being dragged away by the police. They clawed at their captors, fighting against death with hopeless desperation. All day, somewhere, one could hear the sounds of the gruesome chase. The cries and weeping of the unfortunates were mixed with the violent abuse and the wild shouts of the police.*

Where were they being taken? How were they being killed? The Bundists were sure this was the fate of the deported. But how to prove it to the ghetto? Zalman Friedrych, one of the young men in the underground resistance movement and as handsomely blond as Hitler's dream Aryan, was assigned to find out. He stole out of the ghetto and made his way to Sokolov, where he learned that a new branch railroad led to Treblinka. In Sokolov he found another comrade, Azriel Wallach, who had just escaped from a work detail at Treblinka. Wallach told him that all the Jews brought to Treblinka were unloaded from the trains, made to undress, and were then led into gas chambers and killed.

Friedrych returned to Warsaw. The Bund published the terrible facts at once in *Storm*, again warning the Jews not to be deceived: "Do not let them destroy you! Do not give yourselves voluntarily into the hands of your executioners!"

After the first week of deportations, the Germans began entering factories and grabbing workers on the job, sometimes taking out the whole shop. The pretense of selection was dropped. Everyone was in danger, and with the warning in *Storm*, few Jews reported voluntarily for deportation now. The Nazis played on their extreme hunger. Jews were offered a big loaf of bread and a tin of marmalade if they would come in themselves. Feigele Wladka, a member of the Bundist youth and active in the resistance, watched them report.

> They are loaded with sacks, baskets, suitcases; they drag with them the last remnants of their poor belongings, and they are all marching in the same direction towards the Umschlagplatz. . . . Some of them are walking slowly, with drooping heads; others move nervously ahead, with unsteady frightened eyes, seemingly in a hurry, as if they were afraid of being forced to go back. . . . Scarcely anyone in the ghetto is surprised at this quiet, resigned marching. From the hiding places and the shops people look at them with deep sorrow, sometimes mixed with a feeling of admiration. . . . "They have found the strength to take a decision." . . . Crushed under the burden of ghetto life, shriveled or swollen from starvation, haunted by the constant fear of being seized, these Jews could no longer go on with their fight. . . .

One of the Bund fighting group, Marek Edelman, was among the Jews waiting in the *Umschlagplatz*. He saw many retreat into the empty hospital building next door, and finding the toilets locked, relieve themselves where they could. The guards ran after them, revolvers ready.

The air is dreadfully sticky, the stench unbearable. I am leaning against the wall in a state of numbness. . . . On the dirty grey wall the design of a heart pierced by the cupid's arrow has been carved awkwardly with a pocketknife. The inscription says, "Blima and Chilek, August 1942" . . . Night is falling. . . . Somewhere near a child is crying. The whining gets on our nerves. The mother rises from the floor and walks toward the door. She passes a window. At the same moment a shot cracks from behind the window. The woman slowly slips down onto the filthy, spittle-covered floor. She is dead. . . .

At night some of the boldest take their chance. They sneak through the halls. At the height of the fifth floor there is a gangplank leading to the roof of the neighboring house on Niska Street. . . . Below, there is a guard watching the courtyard. The first of the fugitives puts his foot on the plank. Now he is walking. The guard fires. The man, pierced by bullets, falls down. The rest of them scuttle down into the halls. On their way they run into the guards. Violent beating starts now, hitting with rifle butts, the crushing of bones. The wounded, lacerated people, blood-spattered, choking and spitting, return to the Umschlagplatz. . . .

Somebody is reaching for poison. He swallows it, washing it down with a little water carefully prepared in a cruet. It was well hidden. It was not discovered during the examination. The man takes the poison in front of all the people. Nobody interferes. He is passing away. He is delivered. . . .

On a hot Wednesday morning early in August, the Nazis came for the children in Janusz Korczak's orphanage in the Warsaw ghetto. Trained as a neurologist and pediatrician, Dr. Korczak was also widely respected as an educator and an author of children's books. He had founded this home for children without parents and given his life to their care. It was in the middle of breakfast that the police ran in, yelling, "All Jews out! Quickly! Quickly!" The 200 children began moving quietly to the stairs, one of them picking up the green flag of their home. Dr. Korczak, who was ill and weak, suffering from a damaged heart, could have stayed behind, with his physician's exemption. But he stood between the Germans and the children.

Down below, on the street, Hillel Seidman happens to be in the crowd gathered to watch. He sees the long line formed in front of the orphanage on Siska Street.

> A long procession, children, small, tiny, rather precocious, emaciated, weak, shriveled and shrunk. They carry shabby packages; some have schoolbooks, notebooks under their arms. No one is crying.
>
> Slowly they go down the steps, line up in rows, in perfect order and discipline, as usual. Their eyes are turned towards the doctor. They are strangely calm; they feel almost well. The doctor is going with them, so what do they have to be afraid of? They are not alone; they are not abandoned.
>
> Dr. Korczak busies himself with the children with a sober earnestness. He buttons the coat of one child, ties up a package of another, or straightens the cap of a third. Then he wipes off a tear which is rolling down the thin little face of a child. . . .
>
> The procession starts out . . . marching quietly and orderly to the place of their untimely doom. The children are calm, but inwardly they must feel it; they must sense it intuitively. Otherwise how could you explain the deadly seriousness on their pale little faces? But they are marching quietly in orderly rows, calm and earnest, and at the head of them is Janusz Korczak.

That same summer, the Germans were demanding 50,000 Jews from the so-called free zone of southern France, whose capital was Vichy. Pierre Laval, a pro-Nazi and the real power in the Nazi-oriented Vichy government, zealously complied. He even proposed that the Germans take all the Jewish children under sixteen. Some of the Jews rounded up were kept in a camp at Drancy, 3 miles outside Paris, waiting for trains bound for

Auschwitz. During the month, 4,000 children who had been left behind by the evacuation of their parents were deported day by day. Georges Wellers describes how it was done:

> On the day of the deportation the children were usually woken at five o'clock in the morning and dressed in the half-light. It was often cold at five o'clock in the morning but nearly all the children went down to the yard very lightly clad. Suddenly aroused from sleep, ill with sleepiness, the littlest ones would begin to cry and, one by one, the others followed their example. They did not want to go down to the yard, struggled and would not let themselves be dressed. Sometimes it happened that a whole roomful of a hundred children, seized with panic and unconquerable terror, no longer responded to the comforting words of the adults who tried vainly to get them to go downstairs. Then the gendarmes were called, who carried the children down, screaming with terror.
>
> In the yard they waited to be called: they often answered wrongly when their names were called out. The older ones held on to the little ones' hands and would not let go of them. There was a certain number of children in each transport added at the end: those whose names were unknown. These were entered on the list by a question mark. It was of no great importance: it was doubtful whether even half of the unfortunate children would withstand the journey. There was no doubt at all that the survivors would be exterminated shortly after their arrival.

In Warsaw, by the end of the summer of 1942, scarcely 65,000 Jews were still alive. The last raids of that period were made on September 21, Yom Kippur. In the lull that followed, leaders of the Zionist and Bundist underground met on the edge of ruined Warsaw with Jan Karski, an agent of the Polish Government-in-Exile, and gave him a message:

> Tell the Polish and Allied governments we are being systematically murdered. Our entire people will be destroyed.

114

*. . . Place this responsibility on the shoulders of the Allies.
Let not a single leader of the United Nations be able to say that
they did not know that we were being murdered in Poland and
could not be helped except from the outside. The democracies
cannot calmly put up with the assertion that the Jewish people
of Europe cannot be saved.*

Five weeks later, with 2 million Jews already murdered, Karski
reported what he had learned to leaders of the British and United
States governments and to Jewish leaders of Europe and America.
Armed with the facts, Shmuel Zygelbojm, the Bund's delegate to
the Polish National Council in London, tried—and failed—to
break through the world's silence. He killed himself.

This is one version of a ballad, sung in many ghettos, which
tells the story of the transports to the death camp at Treblinka.

-≫

*In a kleyn shtetl gants fri fartog
Mentshn tserudert, a geveyn un a klog.
M'loyft vi meshuge halb naket un bloyz,
M'hert a geshrey: "yidn fun shtub aroys!"
Zhandarmen, politsey, ukrainer fil,
Tsu dermordn di yidn, dos is zeyer tsil!
M'shist un men shlogt, a moyre, a shrek,
Men traybt di yidn tsum ban avek.
Bashraybn kon es nit kayn feder,
Vi es dreyen zich di reder,
Men firt di yidn oyf kidesh-hashem,
Kayn treblinke, kayn treblinke.*

*Undzere brider fun yener zayt yam,
Zey konerr nisht filn undzer bitern tam
Zey konen nit filn undzer bitere noyt
Az oyf undz vart yede minut der toyt.
Di milchome vet nemen amol an ek.
Di velt vet derfarn undzer umderherte shrek.
Ongefilt mit veytik iz dos yidishe harts:
Ver vet konen heyln undzer shmarts?
Taychn trern veln rinen,
Ven men vet amol gefinen
Dem grestn keyver fun der velt
In treblinke, in treblinke.*

In a little town early one morning
Frightened people, weeping and wailing,
Running about like mad, half naked and undressed,
A cry is heard: "Jews, get out of the house!"
Gendarmes, police, many Ukrainians,
To kill the Jews, that is their aim!
They shoot, they beat, it's terrible, horrible,
They drive the Jews to the trains.
No pen can ever describe
How the wheels go round and round.
As the Jews are being martyred,
Going, going to Treblinka.

Our brothers across the ocean
Cannot feel our bitter pain.
They cannot feel our bitter anguish
As death lurks over us every moment.
The war will end some day.
The world will realize the unheard-of horror.
Our Jewish heart is filled with pain:
Who will be able to heal our hurt?
Rivers of tears will flow,
When they will find some day
The biggest grave in the world
In Treblinka, in Treblinka.

12

The Blue Tattoo

From Warsaw, Vienna, and Berlin, from Rotterdam, Paris, and Brussels, from Rome, Prague, Athens, Budapest, and Belgrade, the Jews were deported to the killing centers of Poland until almost the last days of the war. At the Auschwitz complex alone, 1¾ million Jews died in less than two years. At Maidanek, 1½ million.

It is hard to envisage the organization it took to accomplish that end so swiftly. But the Germans managed it. At Auschwitz, 7,000 of them were devoted to the task. All told, more than 47,000 people staffed the extermination industry. It took time to train them. It took careful planning to design the killing process and collect the tools and materials for it. It took inventiveness to perfect the proper gas for the mass production of corpses and the capacious furnaces needed to consume them. Think of the book-keeping alone—the millions of Jews processed through each camp, each assigned a number, each number entered in the record, then tattooed on the left arm. A business not without some inconvenience caused by prisoners who did not always do what was expected of them—proceed neatly from the entrance gate to the gas chamber. Some died of hunger, some of disease, some of exhaustion, some of beatings or torture or bullets. And these deviations, too, had to be kept track of.

But the German system was up to it. It was a good civil service, every man and woman in the right place, always ready to carry out orders. There seemed no lack of bureaucrats ready to contribute to the Final Solution. Not that the Germans lacked assistants! No, they did not have to do it all alone. They found help wherever they needed it. Among the people of every nation they occupied—yes, in the ghettos and camps, too. Among the Jews themselves were some who served the "master race" as police, spies, informers, and hangmen.

The people who ran the camps were a mixture of SS with long service to the movement and bureaucrats specialized in administrative work. The guards, who came from SS regiments, were notorious for sadism and corruption.

The inmates were destined to be killed quickly. The only reasons some survived for any length of time were that the gas chambers and the crematoriums were temporarily too crowded, or that a number of inmates were needed as labor for camp construction and maintenance or for war production. Living quarters were primitive and filthy, clothing was rags, and food was a starvation diet. Sickness and epidemics were therefore common and deadly.

The shock of arrival in such a hellhole as Auschwitz was conveyed by Viktor Frankl. A Viennese physician, he was among 1,500 Jews traveling by train for several days and nights to an unknown station. They were told it would surely be some munitions factory where they would do forced labor. Frankl heard the engine's whistle, sounding like a cry for help, and then, he said:

> The train shunted, obviously nearing a main station. Suddenly a cry broke from the ranks of the anxious passengers. "There is a sign, Auschwitz!" Everyone's heart missed a beat at that moment. Auschwitz—the very name stood for all that was horrible: gas chambers, crematoriums, massacres. Slowly, almost hesitatingly, the train moved on as if it wanted to spare its passengers the dreadful realization as long as possible: Auschwitz.
>
> With the progressive dawn, the outlines of an immense camp became visible; long stretches of several rows of barbed wire fences; watchtowers; searchlights; and long columns of

*ragged human figures, grey in the greyness of dawn, trekking
along the straight desolate roads, to what destination we did
not know. There were isolated shouts and whistles of command.
We did not know their meaning. My imagination led me to see
gallows with people dangling on them. I was horrified, but this
was just as well, because step by step we had to become
accustomed to a terrible and immense horror. . . .*

Then the train moved into the station. Voices shouted commands in rough, shrill tones, the doors were flung open, and squads of prisoners with shaved heads and in striped uniforms stormed inside. They took charge of the new arrivals, grabbing their baggage and searching them for smuggled items—gold, silver, jewels. Everything they tried to keep or hide was stripped away and taken to warehouses to be sorted, packed, and sent off to Germany. From one such camp alone, a train of ten cars packed with clothing, shoes, and sacks of women's hair left for Germany every day. It is strange that most Germans claimed not to have known about the camps when they were wearing second-hand clothing with labels from cities all over Europe. Where did they think it came from? The gold teeth and fillings of the dead were melted down and converted into ingots stored in the vaults of the central bank of Germany. The women's hair was combed, cut, spun into thread, and made into industrial felt from which slippers were produced for the sailors in German submarines. Nothing was wasted, everything was turned into profit in this last stage of the looting process.

Over the main gate at Auschwitz was a big sign. It read: "*Arbeit macht frei*"—Labor liberates. Leaving the train, Frankl and the others were told to fall into two lines, men on one side, women on the other, in order to file past a senior SS officer.

*Instinctively, I straightened on approaching the officer. . . .
Then I was face to face with him. He was a tall man who looked
slim and fit in his spotless uniform. What a contrast to us,
who were untidy and grimy after our long journey! He had
assumed an attitude of careless ease, supporting his right elbow*

with his left hand. His right hand was lifted, and with the forefinger of that hand he pointed very leisurely to the right or to the left. None of us had the slightest idea of the sinister meaning behind that little movement of a man's finger, pointing now to the right and now to the left, but far more frequently to the left.

It was my turn. Somebody whispered to me that to be sent to the right would mean work, the way to the left being for the sick and those incapable of work, who would be sent to a special camp. I just waited for things to take their course, the first of many such times to come. . . . The SS man looked me over, appeared to hesitate, then put both his hands on my shoulders. I tried very hard to look smart, and he turned my shoulders very slowly until I faced right, and I moved over to that side.

Passing the first selection, Frankl was sent to a shed where the new arrivals were disinfected. Some naively asked the old prisoners, there as helpers, if they could keep a wedding ring or a medal or a good-luck piece. Frankl tried to take one of the helpers into his confidence.

Approaching him furtively, I pointed to the roll of paper in the inner pocket of my coat and said, "Look, this is the manuscript of a scientific book. I know what you will say, that I should be grateful to escape with my life, that that should be all I can expect of fate. But I cannot help myself. I must keep this manuscript at all costs; it contains my life's work. Do you understand that?"

Yes, he was beginning to understand. A grin spread slowly over his face, first piteous, then more amused, mocking, insulting, until he bellowed one word at me in answer to my question, a word that was ever present in the vocabulary of the camp inmates. "Shit!" At that moment I saw the plain truth and did what marked the culminating point of the first phase of my psychological reaction: I struck out my whole former life.

120

Primo Levi, a Jewish chemist, was deported from Italy to Auschwitz late in 1943. He too passed the first selection and was put in the work camp, Monowitz, where 40,000 prisoners were making a kind of rubber called Buna. On arrival he was stripped naked, his hair was shorn off, and he was then showered and disinfected. Rags and a broken-down pair of boots with wooden soles were thrown at him. Barefoot and naked, with the clothing in his hand, he was made to run 100 yards, over the blue and icy snow of dawn, to a hut where he was allowed to dress. And then he experienced a sensation something like Frankl's.

When we finish, everyone remains in his own corner and we do not dare lift our eyes to look at one another. There is nowhere to look in a mirror, but our appearance stands in front of us, reflected in a hundred livid faces, in a hundred miserable and sordid puppets. We are transformed into the phantoms glimpsed yesterday morning.

Then for the first time we become aware that our language lacks words to express this offense, the demolition of a man. In a moment, with almost prophetic intuition, the reality was revealed to us: we had reached the bottom. It is not possible to sink lower than this, nor could it conceivably be so. Nothing belongs to us anymore; they have taken away our clothes, our shoes, even our hair; if we speak, they will not listen to us, and if they listen, they will not understand. They will even take away our name: and if we want to keep it, we will have to find in ourselves the strength to do so, to manage somehow so that behind the name something of us, of us as we were, still remains.

Levi's number—174517—was tattooed on his left arm in a swift and slightly painful operation. The prisoners stood in an alphabetized line and moved past a man with the short needle jutting out of the pointed tool. Only by showing his number could 174517 get bread and soup. It took many days for the habits of freedom to wear off. He would still look for the time on his wristwatch, only to find his "name" there instead, tattooed in bluish numerals beneath the skin.

When the new arrivals asked questions of the old-timers, they were always given the same replies: You are not at home. This is not a sanitorium. There is no why here. The only way out is up the chimney.

Primo Levi met a boy of about sixteen the first day. He was a Polish Jew working as an ironsmith. They exchanged names but could not go much further in the only tongue they shared, a miserable German. The boy, Schlome, asked the man, Primo:

> "Where is your mother?"
>
> "In Italy." Schlome is amazed: a Jew in Italy? "Yes," I explain as best I can, "hidden, no one knows, run away, does not speak, no one sees her." He has understood; he now gets up, approaches me, and timidly embraces me. The adventure is over, and I feel filled with a serene sadness that is almost joy. I have never seen Schlome since, but I have not forgotten his serious and gentle face of a child, which welcomed me on the threshold of the house of the dead.

In the work camps, people fell into one of two categories, the saved or the drowned, as Levi called them. The struggle to survive was without letup. Everyone was "desperately and ferociously alone." The men who crumbled were called "mussulmen." In a few weeks they would be ashes in a field and crossed-out numbers in a register. They died alone, leaving no trace in the memory.

Those with energy and acuteness—the organizers, the operators, the people who knew how to fight for material advantages and reputation—had a chance to live longer. It was easy to sink, to go under. Only the exceptional survived more than three months. The others were done in before they could adapt themselves. They made up the anonymous mass of the camps.

The exceptional won jobs as kapos (foremen), cooks, nurses, night guards, hut sweepers, superintendents of latrines and showers. Most of them, in Levi's view, became the type developed in a system of slavery when a few slaves are offered a position of privilege for which they must betray their natural solidarity with their comrades. Levi observed what happens to such a man:

> He will be withdrawn from the common law and will become untouchable; the more power that he is given, the more he will be consequently hateful and hated. When he is given the command of a group of unfortunates, with the right of life or death over them, he will be cruel and tyrannical, because he will understand that if he is not sufficiently so, someone else, judged more suitable, will take over his post. Moreover, his capacity for hatred, unfulfilled in the direction of the oppressors, will double back, beyond all reason, on the oppressed; and he will only be satisfied when he has unloaded onto his underlings the injury received from above.

How such a kapo could behave was described by Nathan Sienicki, one of the Jews deported from France to Auschwitz:

> Our job was to carry planks and panels of wood for the construction of new huts. Our boss was a Polish kapo called Rene, whose number was 25. He was a common criminal and wore the letter "M" on his chest, which distinguished him as a murderer. . . . His cruelty was unbelievable. He would beat us without stopping and force us to run on the job. Every morning we started out with 120 people in his group, but more than half would be dead before the day was over. An average of 70 people a day . . .

Most of the prisoners, said Levi, could rely only upon their own strength to survive. To survive without the loss of dignity and the death of conscience was given to very few. Levi learned how quickly one's own moral world could be given up when hunger swamped the spirit.

> A fortnight after my arrival I already had the prescribed hunger, that chronic hunger unknown to free men, which makes one dream at night, and settles in all the limbs of one's body. I

have already learnt not to let myself be robbed, and in fact if
I find a spoon lying around, a piece of string, a button which
I can acquire without danger of punishment, I pocket them and
consider them mine by full right. On the back of my feet I
already have those numb sores that will not heal. I push
wagons, I work with a shovel, I turn rotten in the rain, I
shiver in the wind; already my own body is no longer mine: my
belly is swollen, my limbs emaciated, my face is thick in the
morning, hollow in the evening; some of us have yellow skin,
others grey. When we do not meet for a few days, we hardly
recognize each other.

How did it happen that Primo Levi was one of the handful to
live to tell his story? He said it was because he chanced to meet
Lorenzo. Lorenzo was an Italian civilian worker, not a prisoner,
who brought him a piece of bread and the remainder of his own
ration every day for six months. He gave him a vest of his own,
full of patches. He wrote a postcard for him, mailed it to Italy,
and brought him a reply.

For all this he neither asked nor accepted any reward,
because he was good and simple and did not think that one did
good for reward. . . . However little sense there may be in
trying to specify why I, rather than thousands of others, managed to survive the test, I believe that it was really due to
Lorenzo that I am alive today; and not so much for his material
aid as for his having constantly reminded me by his presence, by
his natural and plain manner of being good, that there still
existed a just world outside our own, something and someone
still pure and whole, not corrupt, not savage, extraneous to
hatred and terror; something difficult to define, a remote
possibility of good, but for which it was worth surviving. . . .
Thanks to Lorenzo, I managed not to forget that I myself was
a man.

Nor was he the only one not to forget. Levi told of the Greek
Jews:

124

Those admirable and terrible Jews of Salonika, tenacious, thieving, wise, ferocious and united, so determined to live, such pitiless opponents in the struggle for life, those Greeks who have conquered in the kitchens and in the yards, and whom even the Germans respect and the Poles fear. They are in their third year of camp, and nobody knows better than they what the camp means. They now stand closely in a circle, shoulder to shoulder, and sing one of their interminable chants. . . . Their amazing consciousness of the survival of at least a potential human dignity made of the Greeks the most coherent national nucleus in the Lager [camp], and in this respect, the most civilized.

Wachsmann was another man Levi remembered from his barracks in Auschwitz. He had been a *melamed*, or teacher, in the *cheder*, or elementary Hebrew school, of his Galician village, and famed as a healer, too. "Nor am I far from believing it," said Levi, "when I think that this thin, fragile and soft figure has managed to work for two years without falling ill and without dying, but on the contrary is lit up by an amazing vitality in actions and words and spends long evenings discussing Talmudic questions incomprehensibly in Yiddish and Hebrew with Mendi, who is a modernist rabbi."

Sometimes, in the long winter nights, a *badchen*, or storyteller, would come secretly into the barracks, look around cautiously, then sit down on Wachsmann's bunk. At once a small crowd would gather, silent and attentive.

He chants an interminable Yiddish rhapsody, always the same one, in rhymed quatrains, of a resigned and penetrating melancholy (but perhaps I only remember it so because of the time and the place that I heard it?); from the few words that I understand, it must be a song that he composed himself, in which he has enclosed all the life of the Lager in minute detail. Some are generous and give the storyteller a pinch of tobacco or a needleful of thread; others listen intently but give nothing.

Many survivors tell of the same dream, a dream they dreamed many times in the death camps. The elements are always the same. The dreamer is at home with his family, telling them of what has happened in the camp. It is an intense pleasure to be there, among loved ones, and to have so much to tell them. But as the dreamer recounts his experiences, he notices his listeners are not following him. They act indifferent, they interrupt to talk among themselves of other things; it is as if the dreamer is not there. Finally the listeners leave without saying a word to the dreamer.

Awake, the dreamer feels a desolation that is unbearable. It is anguish in its pure state. The pain of each day, suffered again in the night.

13

Zyklon B

And what of death itself in the camps? The death they were designed for, death by gas? In Auschwitz the Jews were killed by a product called Zyklon B. It was hydrogen cyanide, efficient in large rooms. It was made into bluish pellets, which were packed into small canisters. Poured through openings in the ceilings of the killing chambers, the Zyklon turned into gas and did its job.

Zyklon was manufactured by the Dessauer Works and was sold not only for killings but to fumigate ships and buildings and disinfect clothing. The SS bought it for the death camps. SS First Lieutenant Kurt Gerstein handled the payments. Gerstein, thirty-four when the war began, had been trained as a mining engineer. He was also a national official of the YMCA in Germany, in charge of a special program in biblical studies. He joined the Nazi movement when he was young but soon became disillusioned because of its war against the Christian Church. For spreading anti-Nazi propaganda, he was sent to a concentration camp in 1936. Released, he was admitted to the SS, which he joined, he said, in order to expose it to the world. In the summer of 1942 the SS sent him to the Polish death camp called Belzec, to deliver some experimental Zyklon B. There he witnessed the mass extermination of Polish Jews by carbon monoxide.

He tried to tell the Pope's representative in Berlin what he had seen, believing that if the truth were known, the German people would rise up. But he was turned away. Then he wrote a report of his experience and asked the office of the Archbishop of Berlin to forward it to the Pope. On the train returning from Belzec, he had met a Swedish diplomat stationed in Berlin, and stayed up all night to tell him the terrible story. The diplomat sent a report to Sweden, but the Swedish government did not publish the report or forward it to the Allies until the war was over. Even the Dutch resistance movement, which learned Gerstein's story, refused to disclose it, because "nobody would believe it."

What did Gerstein see at Belzec? The following is taken from his own handwritten account:

> . . . In the hot August weather the whole place smelt like the plague and there were millions of flies everywhere. Right by the small two-track station there was a large shed, the so-called cloakroom, with a large counter where valuables were handed over. Then there was a room containing about 100 chairs—the barber's room. Then an outdoor path under birch trees with a doubled barbed-wire fence on the left and right, with the sign: "To the inhalation and bathrooms." In front of us a sort of bathhouse with geraniums, then a few steps, and then three rooms each on the right and left . . . with wooden doors like garages. In the rear wall, scarcely visible in the darkness, large sliding doors. On the roof, as a "witty little joke," the Star of David . . .

Early the next morning he saw the train come in: 45 cars carrying 6,700 people, of whom 1,450 were already dead on arrival. Children looked out the barred windows, their faces pale, their eyes filled with the fear of death. When the train stopped, Ukrainian guards tore open the doors and whipped the people out onto the platform. All had to strip naked and give up their clothes, shoes, valuables, spectacles, artificial limbs, and their hair.

> Then the procession started to move. With a lovely young girl at the front. They all walked along the path, all naked, men, women, and children. . . . Mothers with their babies

at the breast came up, hesitated, and entered the death chambers. A sturdy SS man stood in the corner and told the wretched people in a clerical tone of voice: "Nothing at all is going to happen to you! You must take a deep breath in the chambers. That expands the lungs. This inhalation is necessary because of illness and infection." When asked what was going to happen to them, he answered, "Well, of course, the men must work, building houses and roads, but the women don't have to work. Only if they want to, they can help with the housework or in the kitchen."

This gave some of these poor people a glimmer of hope that lasted long enough for them to take the few steps into the chambers without resisting. The majority realized—the smell told them—what their fate was to be. So they climbed the steps and then they saw everything. . . . They hesitated, but they went into the gas chambers, pushed on by those behind them, or driven by the leather whips of the SS. Most of them without saying a word. A Jewess of about forty, with eyes blazing, called down upon the heads of the murderers the blood being spilt here. Hauptmann Wirth personally gave her five or six lashes in the face with his riding whip. Then she too disappeared into the chamber. Many people were praying. . . .

The chambers filled. . . . People were standing on each other's feet. . . . The SS forced as many in together as was physically possible. The doors closed. Meanwhile the others were waiting outside in the open air, naked. . . . Twenty-five minutes went by. . . . Many were now dead. One could see that, through the little glass window through which the electric light lit up the chamber for a moment. After 28 minutes only a few were still alive. At last, after 32 minutes everyone was dead.

Men of the work squad opened the wooden doors from the other side. . . . The dead were standing upright like basalt pillars, pressed together in the chambers. There would not have been room to fall down or even to bend over. One could see the families even in death. They were still holding hands, stiffened to death, so that it was difficult to tear them apart in order to clear the chamber for the next load. The corpses were thrown *out—wet with sweat and urine, soiled with excrement, menstrual blood on their legs. Children's bodies flew through the air. There was no time to lose. The whips of the Ukrainians whistled down on the backs of the work squad. Two dozen dentists opened the mouths with hooks and looked for gold. Gold on the right, without gold on the left. Other dentists used pliers and hammers to break gold teeth and crowns out of the jaws. . . . The naked corpses were carried in wooden barrows just a few meters away to pits.*

At Belzec, death by monoxide gas took much too long. Rudolf Höss, the SS commandant of Auschwitz, preferred Zyklon B, because it worked faster—in 3 to 15 minutes, depending upon climatic conditions. The most efficient way of disinfecting the world of Jews was the goal of his Party. As Himmler said, "Anti-Semitism is the same as delousing. Getting rid of lice is not a question of ideology; it is a matter of cleanliness. In just this same way anti-Semitism for us has not been a question of ideology but a matter of cleanliness." Once he told his co-workers that the elimination of the Jews "is a page of glory in our history."

The disposal of the bodies was another problem for German ingenuity to solve. At first the bodies were buried in mass graves in the woods. But the decaying corpses left odors that spread for miles, and when the rate of killing increased, the space needed for graves was enormous. Worse, mass graves were evidence of mass killings. So cremation, first in small ovens and then in giant crematoriums, was tried. By 1944, transports came so fast that over 10,000 Hungarian Jews were being gassed per day, and 20,000 Lodz Jews. The ovens couldn't process that many bodies. At Auschwitz they turned to burning the corpses in open pits. This proved to be the cheapest and most efficient method. As Raul Hilberg says, "it took millennia in the development of Western culture" to reach this unlimited capacity for human destruction. The record at Auschwitz was 34,000 people killed and destroyed in 24 hours, through continuous day and night shifts.

In the name of "medical science" the Nazis made special use of the doomed Jews. The victims of these experiments numbered in the hundreds of thousands. Only a handful survived to tell the story at the Nuremberg Trials of the Nazis after the war.

The origin of this practice went back many years. It began on January 2, 1934, when Nazi laws were adopted for the sterilization of the "unfit." Who was to decide who was unfit? "Without the smallest pity," Hitler said that year, he could eliminate millions among the "inferior races that breed like vermin." On the day World War II began, he had launched a program to eliminate "unfit" Aryans. He signed an order allowing doctors to give "mercy deaths" to the "incurably sick." Carbon-monoxide chambers were built to carry out this "euthanasia program." Between December 1939 and August 1941, about 50,000 to 60,000 Germans—children and adults—were secretly killed by lethal injections or in gassing installations designed to look like shower rooms. It was a foretaste of Auschwitz. The victims were taken from the medical institutions and put to death. Their relatives were never consulted or told what had happened. They were simply sent the ashes, never the body, and warned not to demand explanations or to "spread false rumors." It was impossible to squelch suspicion. In December 1940 the Vatican condemned the "mercy killings" as "contrary to both natural and divine law." Two German bishops and a cardinal also spoke up, protesting the gassing of fellow Germans. (They are not known to have protested when non-German Christians or Jews were the victims.) Hitler stopped the gassing in Germany almost at the moment he began it, on a vastly greater scale, in Poland.

There were two types of medical experiments. One was for the usual goals of medical research: to test a drug, a serum, a treatment, a hypothesis. But the Nazis did not rely on volunteer subjects; they forced the camp prisoners to undergo the tests. The German air force, for example, wanted to carry out high-altitude tests on humans, but because the tests were so dangerous, nobody would volunteer. They tried monkeys; that proved unsatisfactory. So air force doctors asked Himmler to put human beings at their disposal. "Gladly," he replied. Jews at the Dachau camp were chosen and locked into the special chamber the air force had provided; then the pressure was altered to simulate atmospheric conditions at extra high altitudes. Eighty died in the "sky ride machine," as the victims called it, and another 129 were killed after "survival" of these experiments.

Freezing experiments were carried out next. Prisoners were forced to stand naked out-of-doors from 9 to 14 hours in below-freezing temperatures. Then they were "warmed up" in a variety of ways, including the use of the most obscene sadism, to see at what point they showed vital life signs. The victims either died in the tests or were killed immediately afterward. (One of the most prominent Nazi scientists who gave conceptual guidance to the tests was Dr. Hubertus Strughold. He came to the United States after the war to pioneer in the development of American space medicine.)

It might be a German army doctor doing research on jaundice or a German chemical company testing a drug against typhus. They all came to the SS for permission to draw upon its huge supply of doomed Jews. Of course each request was for "habitual criminals" as experimental subjects. That was a blind for the conscience. For the choice would inevitably fall upon the "race-defiling Jewish habitual criminals."

Many experiments had nothing to do with attempts to heal the sick. They were experiments in killing; human guinea pigs were used to find out how to widen the destruction process, how to cut down on or get rid of "undesirable, inferior" populations, such as Jews and Gypsies. X rays were used on the sexual organs of young Jewish men to test new methods for mass sterilization. Castration of men was tried at both Auschwitz and Ravensbruck. Chemical irritants were inserted in the uteri of Jewish women to render them sterile, and 300 who did not die from this were then gassed.

All such experiments led to nothing except the deaths of the victims. The tests proved that the racial theory of inferior beings was a poison that had no limit to its destructiveness.

What kind of physician would take part in such work? Professor Johann Kremer was an SS doctor at Auschwitz. He had been a professor of anatomy at the University of Munich before the war. His diary entries for 1942 reveal something of his mentality. On September 2, he witnessed execution by gas for the first time; 918 Jews from France were killed.

> After what I have seen today, Dante's Inferno seems almost a comedy.

On September 5, he was present when 800 sick women were removed from the camp hospital and exterminated.

> Horror of horrors. Thils was right when he told me that here we were at the world's anus.

The next day, Sunday, he noted:

> We had an excellent lunch today—tomato soup, half a chicken and roast potatoes, cake and delicious vanilla ice cream.

On September 9, he was even happier.

> Received the highly welcome information that I was divorced from my wife on the first of this month. I see colors again: a black curtain has been lifted from my life!

Then, with no change of tone:

> Later in my capacity as doctor, was present at the punishment by whipping of 8 prisoners and an execution by small-bore rifles. Was given soap flakes and two bars of soap.

On September 20:

> This Sunday afternoon from three to six o'clock listened to a concert given by the camp orchestra in beautiful sunshine. Conducted by conductor of the Warsaw State Opera. Eighty musicians. For dinner there was roast pork. For supper baked tench.

BOOK THREE

Spirit of Resistance

14

To Die with Dignity

Three times a week little Sima smuggled Jews out of the Minsk ghetto, evading the SS guards, and led them to the forests of Staroje-Sielo, 50 kilometers away.

Who was Sima? We know about her underground work from the memoirs of Jacob Greenstein, a partisan (an anti-Nazi fighting behind the lines) in the Minsk region.

> Sima was a twelve-year-old girl with blonde hair, blue eyes, and dimples that showed when she talked. Her parents perished in the first German pogrom. In the beginning Sima lived outside the ghetto and carried out important assignments for the underground party committee. Later when we began to lead Jews out of the ghetto, Smolar brought the little girl to the ghetto and she became our contact with the forest.
>
> No assignment was too difficult for Sima. Before going out on a mission, she listened carefully to the given instruction; then she would repeat what she was told, trying hard not to miss a single word. Her small pistol was always in the special pocket sewn into her coat. Before starting out, she would always point to it and say, "Don't worry, the Fritzes will not take me alive."
>
> On cold winter nights Sima would sneak out of the ghetto through an opening beneath the barbed wire fence. She returned to the ghetto through the cemetery. There were times

when she did not succeed in getting into the ghetto at night. When this happened, she would spend the night, hungry and cold, in some bombed-out building, and remain there through-out the next day. At dusk, when the Jews returned from work, she would stealthily join their column, and together with them enter the ghetto. After the liquidation of the Minsk ghetto, Sima participated in the combat operations of the partisan detachment.

Sima had an indomitable will to live. She resisted the Nazis, and she survived. Later, when the Germans, now losing the war, were driven out in summer, 1944, Sima marched through Minsk in the front ranks of the partisans. Hers was one of the many forms of resistance to Hitler's persecution. Wherever there was oppression, resistance of some kind emerged. The watchword of the Jewish resistance was: "Live and die with dignity!" And despite the greatest terror, hunger, and privation, Jews upheld that watchword. They did not want simply to vanish silently from the earth.

Acts of resistance were countered by the Nazis with a violence almost beyond belief. In 1941, a group of Dutch Jews dared to attack German police in Amsterdam. Hannah Arendt reports their punishment:

Four hundred thirty Jews were arrested in reprisal and they were literally tortured to death, first in Buchenwald and then in Mauthausen. For months they died a thousand deaths, and every single one of them would have envied his brethren in Auschwitz and even in Riga and Minsk. There exist many things considerably worse than death, and the SS saw to it that none of them was ever very far from their victims' minds and imagination.

Under such conditions, those who conducted an organized and armed resistance were a minority. That even such a minority existed was a miracle. The right question to ask, Elie Wiesel has said, is not: Why didn't *all* the Jews fight? but How did *so many* of them?

Another question to examine is: What was the degree of resistance among non-Jews? Hitler's armies swept over most of Europe with incredible speed. Everyone attributed it to the superior power of the German military forces. The vanquished nations, all of them, had trained and equipped armies. The Jews had nothing. The Nazis killed myriads of people in the parts of Russia they occupied, a territory whose population greatly outnumbered the German troops. How much resistance did Hitler encounter there? Millions of Russian captives were transported to German prisons and labor camps and treated so brutally that 5 million of them died. How many riots or acts of resistance took place among them? Yet no one accuses them of going like sheep to slaughter. No, the vast majority in the prisoner-of-war camps behaved much as did the civilians in the occupied countries. They were inert, passive; they did what they were ordered to do, hoping simply to survive. A minority chose to collaborate with the Nazis. Another minority chose to actively resist.

The purpose here is not to criticize or demean others, only to indicate how hard it is for anyone to resist a ruthless totalitarian power which commands modern weapons and employs elaborate means to crush opposition.

Even so, throughout occupied Europe, when the terrible truth about the Final Solution became clear to some Jews, they urged the others to resist physically. Realists accepted the fact that Hitler meant to annihilate every Jew in Europe, but the majority of Jews could not believe this would happen. Partly because the Germans shrouded their evil work in utter secrecy. Partly because the Germans used many forms of deception to confuse and mislead their victims. And perhaps most importantly, because the very idea of mechanical and systematic mass murder struck most people—everywhere in the world—as utterly inconceivable. It seemed infinitely different from the earlier examples of what came to be known as genocide. It went far beyond the reach of the human imagination. As Dr. Louis de Jong, a Dutch historian of the Holocaust, once said, "Our mind, once having grasped the facts, immediately spewed them out as something utterly alien and unnaturally loathsome." A group of Jehovah's Witnesses, who were put in the death camp at Birkenau, by the side of the gas chambers and crematoriums, said later, "One day we would believe our own eyes; the next day we would simply refuse to do so." Another Hollander, Emile Franken, was one of a group in Birkenau which saw the crematorium chimneys smoking day in and day out. But the inmates, "the people themselves," he said, "pretended that the place was a brickyard or a soap factory. This mass delusion lasted for four weeks." He was the only one among them who could accept the unbearable truth.

The gas chambers spelled death not only for oneself but for husband, wife, children, grandparents, relatives, friends. How many among the millions who died in them could face that awesome truth? Professor de Jong concludes:

> We should be committing an immense historical error, were we to dismiss the many defense mechanisms employed by the victims—not constantly, mind you, but by way of intermittent distress signals—as mere symptoms of blindness or foolishness; rather did these defense mechanisms spring from deep and inherent qualities shared by all mankind: a love of life, a love of family, a fear of death, and an understandable inability to grasp the reality of the greatest crime in the history of mankind, a crime so monstrous . . . that even its perpetrators (the sadists and other perverts among them excepted) were unable to dwell on their activities for too long.

As some Jews became convinced that their people were doomed, the natural question to ask was: How then shall we die? One answer was to frustrate the enemy by not making it easy for him: Do not commit suicide; stay alive as long as you can. The simple act of living on became a form of passive resistance. Many expressed that resistance by carrying on their traditional religious life—praying, singing, studying the Talmud, observing the Holy Days—and their cultural activities in the ghettos. Others hid from the enemy as long as they could. Some bore children as if to say, No matter what you do, the generations will go on.

Other Jews, who began to understand that Nazi terror was a totally different order of life, chose more active ways of responding to it. They felt it was hopeless to rely on legal methods in such a morally criminal system. So people learned how to use bribery, smuggling, forgery, theft, spying, sabotage, violence. They saw these as weapons of defense against a power committed to their destruction. They bribed the enemy; they smuggled food and people; they stole bread and guns; they forged papers—birth and baptismal certificates, residence cards, ration cards, work cards, registration forms, passports. They planted spies in the enemy's ranks; they sabotaged war production; they blew up trains and bridges and buildings; they shot and stabbed and poisoned Hitlerites.

The essential fact is that one can resist in a great many ways, by acting and yes, sometimes, by refusing to act. Armed fighting, for those physically able to undertake it, will usually do the most damage to the enemy. And, of course, there were armed battles. That aspect of Jewish resistance—apart from the Warsaw Ghetto Uprising—is almost ignored in the earlier accounts of the Holocaust. One reason for the neglect is the fact that historians based themselves largely on the captured Nazi documents, which gave only a one-sided version of what happened. As the years pass, documentation of resistance by the Jews increases in many languages, especially Yiddish. This includes not only memoirs written during the Holocaust and after liberation but depositions of witnesses, records of trials, and thousands of oral interviews with survivors all over the world.

Some historians, such as Raul Hilberg, argue that the "Jews of all regions and all classes failed to resist in significant measure throughout the destruction process." It all depends upon the definition of resistance. Hilberg limits it to armed fighting. He excludes bribery, ransom, and rescue as only "alleviation," and flight and hiding he calls simply "evasion." But the resistors themselves and some of the research organizations devoted to the study of the Holocaust (Yad Vashem in Israel and YIVO Institute for Jewish Research in New York) commonly include as honorable examples of resistance what Professor Hilberg would leave out.

To account for his view, Hilberg and others claim that the Jewish tradition of 2,000 years in the Diaspora was one of non-resistance to and compliance with oppression. That view is countered by many who interpret Jewish history differently. A Polish Jewish writer, M. Edin, has this to say:

> Some naive researchers and publicists discovered the Jews for the first time in the ghetto barricades. These writers say that the Jews had not fought since Maccabean times . . . that only in the presence of death in the ghetto did the Jew take to arms. This is not true. We shall not discuss here the fighting tradition of the Jewish masses of the nineteenth century, beginning with exploits of Berek Yoselevich's division [in the Polish uprising of 1832]. But only a superficial acquaintance with the participation of the Jewish workers and the Jewish intelligentsia in the labor movement of Poland and Russia from its inception down to the Nazi attack is enough to refute this view. For the Jews manifested heroism not only in cases of individuals like Shulman, Hirsh Leckert, Naftali Botwin and Engel, but even more importantly, on the part of the Jewish working masses as a whole. From this working class tradition and from the intellectual and moral training and ideology of the working class movement did men and women like Joseph Levartovsky, Andjei Schmidt and a legion of Jewish resistance heroes, known and unknown, draw strength in this most tragic period. . . .

Here the writer is stressing one of the two traditions in Jewish history—the tradition of physical resistance to persecution. That pattern of resistance, as he implies, came out of a historical experience developed over a long period of time. Each nation has traditions and values shaped by its own past. America and France have had a revolutionary tradition since the late eighteenth century. The Poles, too, beginning with the insurrection of 1794 and the many that broke out during the next hundred years. And the

142

Yugoslavs, since their struggles against the Turks. The Czechs took a somewhat different course, after the terrible defeat of the Hussite rebellion in the fifteenth century. Under Hapsburg domination they developed methods of passive resistance which they later used against the Nazis.

Another critic of Hilberg is the historian Reuben Ainsztein. His 900-page study of Jewish resistance in Nazi-occupied Eastern Europe thoroughly documents all aspects of Jewish action in defense of life and dignity. He asserts that in charging Hitler's victims with cowardice, Hilberg has laid Jewish behavior to a history of passivity in the Diaspora. Ainsztein refutes this by a fresh examination of the Jews in history, showing them to have been neither born victims nor born martyrs. He presents a detailed survey of the Diaspora Jew as soldier, seaman, corsair, merchant-adventurer, and explorer. The tradition of the Jewish fighter in antiquity never died, he says. "The role of the fighter . . . in ensuring Jewish survival is . . . at least as important as that of the religious martyr."

Jewish methods of resistance to oppression have not been uniform. Dispersed throughout many varying cultures, the Jews were inevitably affected by their interactions with their host societies. The intellectuals, the assimilated part of the middle class, and the working class absorbed the traditions and values of those nations. What about the Jews who maintained their religious orthodoxy? Philip Friedman, a Jewish historian born in Galicia, who was active in the anti-Nazi underground in Poland, explains how their traditions influenced the question of resistance:

> . . . The large mass of Orthodox Jews, particularly in Eastern and Southeastern Europe, had quite a different attitude to those problems. Whereas most other nations have legacies of heroism in which heroism means physical and military prowess, in the case of Orthodox Jewry the concept of heroism is interwoven with the idea of spiritual courage, of sacrifice for the sake of religion, known in Hebrew as Kiddush Hashem (Sanctification of God's Name). This was the main form of resistance carried on by the Orthodox Jews. It was a resistance

stemming from religious inspiration and it contained a deeply rooted ancestral heritage epitomized by the saying, "not by force but by the strength of the spirit."

This attitude had been maintained during many centuries of religious persecution. Its essence is epitomized in the idea that the evil of the world should not be fought and cannot be defeated by physical force, because the struggle between good and evil will be decided elsewhere, by Divine Providence; it will by no means be decided by physical warfare. In accordance with this view, the true weapon is the weapon of conscience, prayer, religious meditation and devotion, and not armed resistance.

The Orthodox Jew did not believe that it was possible or even desirable to resist the Nazis in any other way. They believed that the recital of a chapter of the Psalms would do more to affect the course of events than the killing of a German —not necessarily immediately but in the infinite course of mutual relations between the Creator and His creatures.

"Not by force but by the strength of the spirit . . . " An example of what that means comes from an eyewitness account of what happened in the Polish town of Dabrowa when the Germans found Rabbi Isaac and his Hasidic disciples hiding in an underground shelter. The Nazis drove them to the local Jewish cemetery. Waiting for the Germans in their hideout, the Hasidim were dressed in their praying shawls and had a bottle of vodka which they managed to bring to the cemetery. There, facing their executioners, as the account goes, "they drank *lechayim* (to life) to each other, held hands and began to dance, and were shot down as they danced. The Germans were so enraged by the scene, which they had failed to prevent, that they slit the Jews' bellies and trampled on them until the bowels came out."

Keeping these traditions in mind, what can be learned from the history of resistance movements? There are basic conditions necessary for their success. One is a favorable place to fight—such as mountains, forests, marshes. These existed in Europe but were denied the Jews because they were locked behind ghetto walls. All their moves could be observed and controlled. To start an underground conspiracy under such conditions and to link it with others was neither easy nor safe. Smuggling weapons into the ghetto required great courage and ingenuity. And getting fighters out of a ghetto—studded with spies and surrounded by guards—and into the forests and mountains was even harder.

That very decision—whether to stay in the ghetto with the mass of Jews or to escape and fight outside—was an agonizing one to make. Many passionate debates took place over the moral issue. Usually they ended with the resistance forces staying inside. They helped the inmates of the ghetto struggle against oppression and then led the fight against the deportations to the death camps. They left only when there was no longer any chance to be useful in the ghetto.

The ghetto Councils, faced with the choice—to resist or not to resist—did not act on a rigid pattern. There were variations, but the end remained the same. In Vilna, the Judenrat did whatever the Germans asked. Its head, Jacob Gens, seems even to have used Jewish police to assist at mass executions. And Gens himself forced the resistance leader Itzik Wittenberg to give himself up to the Nazis. (The Germans killed Wittenberg and two months later, shot Gens.) In Kovno, while the Council seemed to be carrying out Nazi orders, its leader, Dr. Elkhanen Elkes, worked secretly with the resistance; and the Jewish police chief, Moshe Levin, doubled as a resistance leader, smuggling out many young Jews to join the partisans. In Lodz and Warsaw, the Councils opposed resistance. In Lvov, two Council heads heroically refused to collaborate with the Nazis.

The resistance movements in the ghettos challenged the position of those Councils which believed that by working for the Germans, the Jews would save themselves. The partisans of the Vilna ghetto, as early as January 1942, seven months before the deportation of Jews to Treblinka began in Warsaw, published a call which warned that "The fate of the Jews under Hitlerite occupation is total annihilation, regardless of the economic interests of the Germans. Brothers! Away with the illusion that we will

be saved by virtue of economic necessity! . . . The destruction
. . . is a systematic process which sooner or later will include
everyone. . . ."

The historian Isaiah Trunk concludes that "the majority of the
Councils were against the idea of organized resistance." He cites
town after town where the Councils tried by every means to
oppose the resistance movements. There was one Council head,
Moshe Merin of Bedzin-Sosnowiec, who betrayed many young
people to the Nazi executioners and was himself sentenced to
death by the underground movement. Trunk also lists a smaller
number of Councils which supported the resistance. Among the
leaders were such men as Eliyahu Myshkin of Minsk and Abraham
Gefner of Warsaw. In Iwaniska, Chaim Rabinowicz, a rabbi who
was a member of the Council, helped some 300 young people
escape to the woods, where they had a chance to take revenge on
the enemy.

There were Council members who remain controversial figures
today. One such is Adam Czerniakow, head of the Warsaw
ghetto. He committed suicide when the Nazis ordered him to
supply 10,000 Jews a day instead of 6,000. Some hold he was a
martyr, because he killed himself rather than carry out the order.
But the poet Yitkhok Katzenelson, active in the Warsaw resistance, asked, How do you distinguish between handing over 10
rather than 6 Jews? "How many more than 6 are 10? To 6 you
agree, but at 10 you object?"

Trunk reports that, of the some 700 people he has listed who
were members of 404 Councils, 182 were killed before the deportations began, 21 resigned, 13 were dismissed or arrested, 9 committed suicide, 26 died "natural" deaths, 383 were shipped to
death camps, and 86 escaped.

Under such enormous pressure, manipulated by the diabolical
methods of the Nazis, people were understandably deluded. Some
collaborated, some collapsed, some even served as agents of the
Gestapo. What happened under Hitlerism echoed what had happened under czarism a hundred years earlier. In the time of Czar
Nicholas I, the traditional Jewish community councils had been
ordered to supply boys to serve in the army for twenty-five years.

The sons of the rich, the gifted few, and the promising Talmudic scholars escaped service, while the children of the poor and the helpless were seized by the Jewish councils and handed over to the army. There was often the same injustice and inhumanity in the Nazi ghettos. A tiny minority of Jewish officials and racketeers lived (for a time) in relative ease, while the poor carried the heaviest burdens of taxation, forced labor, starvation, and deportation. In his Warsaw-ghetto diary, Emmanuel Ringelblum cried out passionately, "The entire activity of the Jewish Council is one shocking injustice against the poor."

The most useful way to examine the record of the Judenrat might be from the perspective of Jewish history, rather than as a matter of making moral judgments on individuals. The best members of the Jewish Councils meant to save lives. If they collaborated, it was to keep as many Jews as possible alive until the defeat of Germany. But the lesson for the world now is that collaboration only made the Councils accomplices to mass murders. Ber Mark, a historian of the Warsaw Ghetto Uprising, sees the actions of the collaborationist Councils as one of two lines of development in Jewish history:

> One—self-defense, resistance and struggle; the other—accommodation and desertion. One—joining the liberation movements of mankind; the other—fear of the Authority and isolating oneself in a spiritual ghetto. One—an honorable struggle for national rebirth, for national rights, for a free Jewish people among free peoples; the other—pleasing the reactionary ruler, submission to the oppressor, and deserting one's own people. In the conditions of the ghetto this meant: the line of resistance versus the line of the Judenrat.

Whatever its internal problems, and no matter where it operated, the resistance movement needed the friendly help of the non-Jewish populations. Only from them could come essential information, food, shelter for the sick and wounded, and hiding places for partisans and weapons. But in very few Nazi-occupied countries could the Jewish underground find friends among the general populations. The Jews felt themselves terribly alone in their struggle. Even sympathetic non-Jews wavered in their support, fearing the cruel punishment of the Nazis. But more often the local people were indifferent or actively hostile to the Jews. They did not look upon the Jewish cause as their own.

Nor could the Jewish underground count upon the Allied governments fighting Germany or the governments-in-exile from their Nazi-occupied countries for the supply of arms. No country treated the Jewish resistance on equal terms with its own national underground. Whatever weapons the Jews received came too few and too late. They were forced to buy arms through illegal channels, paying black-market prices, or to make their own in small and secret shops. Their weaponry was pathetic against the power of German guns.

As for leadership, the most promising was eliminated early by the Nazis. Hitler's policy of quick arrest, imprisonment, and execution of political and labor leaders, intellectuals, and professionals, including seasoned soldiers of earlier wars, decapitated the potential resistance. It was therefore the Jewish youth organizations of all kinds that became the source of resistance leadership. Denied the experience and example of their elders, they had to learn everything for themselves.

Nevertheless, Jews took part in the resistance in all countries. In two ways: as members of the national resistance movements or as part of the specifically Jewish resistance. In the first case, as Henri Michel, historian of the European resistance movements, points out, they were often the leading spirits in the resistance. In his own country, France, he wrote that the Jews "made the greatest contribution of anybody in proportion to their numbers among the population as a whole." At least a million Jews fought in national armies of the Allies or in the resistance forces, a fact not to be forgotten.

Jewish underground groups were of many political beliefs, each growing and learning on its own, usually with few or no links to other groups. Because the Nazi extermination machine went into high gear so early in the war, the Jewish groups had little time in which to develop. The Nazi mobile killing squads began their work in 1939, and annihilation by gas started in the fall of 1941. Within two years the ghettos of Europe were emptied by death.

Worst of all for members of the Jewish underground was the hopelessness of their fight. They faced total destruction, and they all knew it. They had no homeland they could call their own, no place they could dream of returning to. Members of the non-Jewish resistance fought to win back their political freedom and to live at peace once again in their own homes. That was a simple goal, an end to all this terror, which they could hold in sight. But for the Jews there was no such hope to cherish and struggle for. Their only goal was to die with dignity and honor.

15

I Want to Live

Passive resistance was one of the many forms in which the Jews carried on the struggle against the Nazis. Do not think that because arms were not used, it meant no risk. Out of principle or religious belief, some people would not take up a gun. Yet they suffered and died rather than give in to Nazism. There were the prayer groups who congregated in the ghettos and camps, disobeying German orders not to. Jews lost their lives while rescuing Torah Scrolls from burning synagogues. The Hasidim prayed and sang in ghetto streets, even as the Germans clubbed them down. There were many who acted as Janusz Korczak did when he chose death with his orphanage children rather than accept exemption for himself. In Lodz, an underground group monitored Allied radio broadcasts and spread the news until they were betrayed. Writers and actors dared torture and death to satirize the Nazis in ghetto theaters. Teachers took the same chances when they conducted secret schools for children.

It was in Berlin that one of the most incredibly courageous Jewish resistance groups operated. Incredible because, first, it was formed in the very heart of Hitler's Germany. And second, because most of the 32 members of the group were only eleven to fourteen years of age when Hitler came to power. By the time they became active, the four leaders were nineteen years old. These were two married couples, Herbert and Marianne Baum, and Sala and Martin Kochmann.

The Baum group, as it came to be known, started in 1937 with social gatherings at the home of the Baums at Stralanerstrasse 3. The young people met to hear music and talk. Soon the group began discussing politics and the plight of the Jews. Most of the boys and girls were Zionists; two were Communists.

A year later came *Kristallnacht*. The Nazis put about a thousand young Jews to work in the Siemens electric motor plant in Berlin, segregating them in special departments under slave-labor conditions. Herbert and Martin, classmates at school and now old friends, were among them. With their wives, they decided to set up a secret unit to organize a Jewish resistance group. Herbert was allowed to be the one Jew at Siemens who could speak for the others to the factory overseer in charge of Jews. With his small group, Baum succeeded in recruiting many other young Jewish workers.

During 1939 and 1940, the underground group tried to do cultural work among the city's Jews and to lift the morale of those who had sunk into despair. Baum protested to the factory against the low wages and brutal working conditions of the Jews. But in vain, of course.

The group at Siemens began to draw in Jewish youths from other factories. Early in 1941 a man who had escaped from Buchenwald brought them news of the actions of a Jewish resistance group in the concentration camp, led by Rudi Arndt, a young man well known to Berlin's Jews. He had been murdered by the SS a few months earlier. Arndt's example inspired the Baum group to try bolder resistance actions. When the German-Soviet war began in June 1941, the group gained confidence. They felt the Hitler regime was doomed now and they must do all they could to help speed its end.

They began distributing pamphlets and leaflets against the war and Hitlerism, getting them into homes, offices, and factories. Two young women, non-Jewish office workers, joined the group and helped by typing stencils at home.

At night the young people took terrible chances by posting up their broadsides and painting slogans on the walls. Besides sharing in such work, the members had the responsibility of educating people politically wherever they were, and of raising the morale of the Jews around them.

As the deportation of German Jews continued, Baum procured forged Aryan documents in the hope of saving his group, should they fall victim to mass roundups. It cost a great deal to do this and to buy food for group members who were starving on the pitiful rations allotted Jews. The group had to find funds somewhere. They planned and carried out two daring robberies that produced valuable goods which they were able to exchange for cash.

In May 1942, Goebbels opened an exhibition in Berlin called "The Soviet Paradise." Its aim was to persuade the Germans that the war against Russia was necessary; and it was timed to divert attention from German defeats in the East. The Baum group decided to destroy the exhibition. One night seven of them, led by Herbert and Marianne, entered the hall and started a fire with explosives. They left safely as the flames shot up, destroying part of the exhibit before firemen could arrive.

The Gestapo arrested the seven within a few days, then used the fire as an excuse to round up 500 innocent Jews. The Nazis shot half of them and sent the other half to the Sachsenhausen camp.

Herbert Baum was tortured by the Gestapo and beaten to a bloody pulp. Then they dragged his half-dead body through the Siemens plant and demanded that he identify his accomplices. He refused to betray anyone. The Gestapo then said he had committed suicide, but other prisoners testified later that he had been tortured to death.

By the end of the year, the whole Baum group had been captured. Most were condemned to death by a "people's court" and decapitated. Three of the women were given prison terms and sent to concentration camps, where they all died.

Gestapo records found after the war show that some of the young men and women proudly admitted they had shared in the resistance movement. None expressed regret or asked for mercy. One of them, Lotte Rothholz, said under interrogation: "One must use every opportunity to fight against the present regime. I, personally, am not schooled in politics. . . . But one thing was clear to me: as a Jew I must not lag behind. . . . My ties were and remain with Baum."

Such heroic actions were rare inside Germany but more common outside. In the Lithuanian town of Marcinkonis, the Germans lined up freight cars early one November morning in 1942 and ordered the Jews to board them for deportation. The whole community of 370 Jews refused. Four of the local Jews, in a collective report, described what happened:

> Ahron Kobrovsky, President of the Judenrat, cried out, "Jews, whoever wants to live, let him run where he can! The play is with the devil!" The Jews began to run toward the ghetto fence. . . . The commandant began shooting his automatic pistol in all directions. His subordinates did likewise. Cries of women and children were heard and the groans and rattling sounds of the wounded and dying. Everybody ran from the ghetto. The fence was broken down. The panic and pandemonium in the ghetto was indescribable. There were not a few cases of Jewish men beating the armed murderers with their bare fists and trampling them underfoot. The shooting on every side became intensified. Many dead and wounded fell. Groans and wails filled the air. The Germans did not succeed in catching alive one single Jew, man, woman or child, to throw into the freight cars. One hundred five Jews remained lying dead in the ghetto and outside the enclosure. . . .

Jews sometimes set their ghettos afire when the Nazis came to deport them, and in the confusion that followed, took flight. Escape to the forest was often attempted, or hiding in the homes of Christians. Enormous ingenuity, labor, and daring went into the creation of hiding places. There were tunnels dug to the "Aryan side," breaks made under and over and through ghetto walls, burrows built beneath cellars and around sewers. Whole families shared in this form of resistance to Hitler's sentence of death.

Sabotage was resistance, too. In the Minsk ghetto, members of

the underground who worked in German factories sabotaged production. Jewish tailors stitched uniforms so that they would come
apart, and shoemakers put nails in soles so as to cripple the
wearers. Leather goods and textiles were shipped out with secretly
produced chemicals, introduced at the last minute, which ruined
them for use. The smuggling and other illicit methods used to
gather food are another example of passive resistance. Masses of
Jews did their best to thwart regulations aimed at destroying the
ghetto by hunger.

In the Minsk ghetto the first Judenrat worked closely with the
resistance movement. When the Germans ordered the Council to
collect fur coats for the army's winter campaign, the Judenrat
delivered only half to the Germans. The other half was sent to
the partisans, the resistance fighters in the forest. Trapped finally
by the Nazis, the whole first Judenrat, except for one member,
was publicly executed.

In Kovno, the Jews joining the resistance took this oath:

> I promise to fight with all my powers against the Nazi
> occupation; to endanger their encampments; disrupt their
> transport; burn and blow up bridges; destroy railroads; organize
> and help carry through acts of sabotage at every opportunity
> and under all circumstances, without sparing myself—and when
> necessary, to offer up my life.

It was in that Lithuanian ghetto that Leib Segalov burned
down three huge ammunition and winter-clothing storehouses.
And Yankel Kopelman set fire to a train carrying German rein-
forcements to the front. Two other resistance members, Mayer
Luria and Feivel Forad, were killed while destroying an artillery
train.

No one knows how many survived in bunkers—the underground hiding places in the fields and woods. Sometimes it was
one person alone; sometimes a small group. They depended upon
nearby peasants for food and warnings, or had to forage for themselves, secretly and by night. Moses Feigenbaum, a Polish Jew, was
one of four fugitives who dug a pair of bunkers in an orchard close

to his own town. His mother, wife, child, and sisters had all been killed by the Nazis. Two Polish women and a young farmhand gave the group help. Feigenbaum told their story:

With no possibility of washing regularly, we became filthy and vermin-ridden. Delousing was to be, in fact, an important part of our daily routine. Yet when we had completed our bunkers and lay all day without a lick of work to do, we found we'd have to think of a way to keep busy. To begin with, we decided to make our bunkers more comfortable, to turn them into tiny underground cabins instead of the living graves they were. There was plenty of wood only 6 kilometers away, and we made several nightly forays. . . .

After we had tidied the bunkers and covered the wooden floor and walls with straw mats, it was our turn to clean up: nor did we skimp on soap or water. Finally we changed our underwear. Clean and comfortable at last.. . . . We grew hungry and began to wish for some home cooking. We managed to get hold of a primus stove. . . . There were lots of things for our table in the fine orchards where we were living. . . .

When sleep will not come, you remember the times you hoped for such a hiding place; now that you have it, you are apathetic and only long for death. . . . In the evening we sit around a pot of warm food, talk and play dominoes. By day we read—if there is something to read. When there is nothing else to do, we sleep. Generally, we sleep a great deal. Though our dreams are bad, it is better than being awake. . . . The tedium of our underground existence becomes unendurable at last. So overpowering is my desire to see another face that I decide to tempt fate by visiting my town. . . .

Feigenbaum crawled through deep snowdrifts to reach his town. In the Jewish quarter he found only ruined buildings and empty houses. Every trace of the Jewish cemetery had been destroyed. He learned that the Germans were rapidly retreating before the Russian Army, which would soon be near.

I cannot leave without passing our house. As I draw near,
I seem to hear my father's voice, bidding me welcome. I want
to fall down and kiss the cold stones. But I only stand there,
like a Jew at the Wailing Wall. . . .

Young Abraham Lipser went into hiding, too, but by a different means. He was nineteen when the Germans began to herd Polish Jews into ghettos. With the other six members of his family, who lived in the village of Janow, he was sent to a transit camp. The filthy barracks housed 45,000 Jews. Within seven weeks, 30 percent of them died. One day thousands were picked out and ordered to board trains bound for an unknown station. The Lipser family felt lucky to be together, seated not in one of the cattle cars but in an old passenger coach. Abraham described their departure:

There were tears on my mother's face; my father's lips moved
silently, in prayer. I looked through the battered window; the
camp was behind us. Suddenly the news spread along the
grapevine that we were headed for Auschwitz. I shuddered. SS
guards patrolled the corridor outside. No escape that way. I
looked at my mother, crouching in a corner of our compart-
ment, her face buried in her hands. It seemed as though we had
stopped breathing. Then I began to think: I am young. . . . I
want to live. . . . I must try my luck and jump off this death
train. . . .
I fell back in my seat, laughing like a lunatic. My father shook
his head and motioned me to keep quiet; my mother continued
to weep quietly. Slowly, it grew dark. Suddenly, I rushed to the
window, pulled it open, and threw myself clear. A hail of
bullets from the guns of the guards on top of the train swept to
the right and left of me. I lay motionless. What if the train
should stop? But the train moved on, and now I was alone, with
agonized thoughts of my parents, whom I had left behind. My
knee was bleeding profusely; no matter, I had escaped.
I crawled through a thicket and found myself on the highway

156

outside Janow. Going back would have been sheer folly. But a lifelong friend of my father's—a Gentile—had a farm and homestead nearby and I headed there. The old man stared at me, utterly bewildered. "Is it really you?" he whispered. Murmuring a prayer in Polish, he took me by the hand, and drew me over the threshold. Our situation was precarious. If I were found, my father's friend and all his family would be exterminated. "But," he added, after a moment's reflection, "I'll take that risk." He proposed to dig a hole in the stable, cover it with boards and pile straw and manure on top. "I'll bring you three square meals a day," he said. "You need fattening up badly." I squeezed his hand without a word; but I knew he understood.

Lipser stayed in that dark hole for two years. In 1944, unable to bear the isolation any longer, he left, made his way to Warsaw, obtained a forged passport, and moved through Austria and Italy to Cyprus and, finally, Palestine. He and one brother were the only ones in the family to survive.

May Day, the traditional labor holiday, became the occasion for demonstrating defiance of the Nazi edict against celebrating it. The Polish town of Menzerzyce had a large number of Jewish workers, mostly brushmakers. It had been a center of the Bund before the war. The Germans were constantly carrying out manhunts on the streets to obtain forced labor. Jews lived in daily fear of capture. Despite that, on May Day the workers marched through the town in small, silent groups. They said nothing, sang nothing. But the whole town saw, and took courage from, their extraordinary demonstration.

Golda Cuker was one of the young underground Bundists in Menzerzyce. Married to a brushmaker, she had two little girls. The Germans had taken several hundred men from the town and put them in a labor camp nearby. Because Golda looked like a Pole, her job in the Bund was to make the rounds of the villages to scrounge food for the starving inmates of the labor camp. She also tried to find secret hideouts for Jewish children on the farms of the peasants. One day, while on such a mission, she disappeared. Her younger sister, doing the same work, suffered the same fate.

It is hard to draw the line between passive and active resistance. The Jew in a ghetto garment factory who chose on his own to sabotage German army uniforms was resisting the Nazis. Not with the gun, with the needle. Acts of sabotage carefully prepared and carried out under direction from an underground center were a more effective form of resistance, perhaps, but each act required the same moral courage.

Another distinction to be made between forms of active resistance is between the armed and the unarmed. The young Jews of occupied France offer a superb example of unarmed resistance. After the big roundup of nearly 13,000 Jews on July 16, 1942, there remained thousands of boys and girls between eleven and eighteen who had escaped the police net. Overnight they became outlaws—their families, homes, funds gone. Many joined the French resistance—the men, women, and children who worked to combat the French Nazi-collaborators and the occupying Nazi forces. Within the Jewish Scout Organization, which had been much like any scout movement before the war, was formed a group of youngsters who carried on unarmed resistance work. Called "The Sixth," they organized a network of small shops which forged "Aryan" documents. (One of the boys, Maurice Lobenberg, proved so resourceful, he produced several hundred identity cards a day.) They founded a string of safe hiding places for Jewish children and adults, supplying the fugitives with identity papers. They brought their charges food and clothing and visited them regularly. Much of this work was done for foreign Jews living in France, Jews especially exposed to danger because they could not speak French and had no local connections. "The Sixth" made contacts with the religious orders, Protestant and Catholic clergy, and friendly municipal authorities and police. They worked with professional smugglers to get fugitives safely across the mountains into refuges abroad. They rescued over 3,000 adults and 1,000 children. At a price: of the 88 boys and girls in "The Sixth," 4 were shot to death by the Nazis, and 26 were deported to death camps.

In occupied Belgium, young Jews set fire to a train carrying raw materials to Germany. They raided bureaus which printed meal tickets, acquiring over a quarter million a month that way. In one coup they stole all 275,000 meal tickets carried on a train heading from Brussels to Ghent. Half the tickets they gave to the resistance and to Jews; the rest they sold to get funds for their work.

JEWISH PARTISAN SONG (ZOG NIT KEINMOL)
Words by Hirsh Glick

Translated from the Yiddish by Aaron Kramer

Never say that there is only death for you
Though leaden skies may be concealing days of blue—
Because the hour we have hungered for is near;
Beneath our tread the earth shall tremble: We are here!

From land of palm-tree to the far-off land of snow
We shall be coming with our torment and our woe,
And everywhere our blood has sunk into the earth
Shall our bravery, our vigor blossom forth!

We'll have the morning sun to set our day aglow,
And all our yesterdays shall vanish with the foe,
And if the time is long before the sun appears,
Then let this song go like a signal through the years.

This song was written with our blood and not with lead;
It's not song that birds sing overhead,
It was a people, among toppling barricades,
That sang this song of ours with pistols and grenades.

So never say that there is only death for you.
Leaden skies may be concealing days of blue—
Yet the hour we have hungered for is near;
Beneath our tread the earth shall tremble: We are here!

ZOG NIT KEINMOL

Words by
HIRSH GLIK

16

Ghetto Uprising

Few people realize how widespread armed resistance to the Nazis was in the several hundred ghettos of occupied Europe. The Jewish underground organizations made the preparations in many places, but in others the rebellions were spontaneous. Tuczno, a small town in the Ukraine, was one such place. The Jews of all the neighboring towns were wiped out by the Germans with the help of the anti-Semitic Ukrainians. But Tuczno's Jews were spared for a time because many worked in the two factories producing badly needed leather and cloth. Late in the summer of 1942, the Germans ordered a ghetto wall to be built around the town's 3,000 Jews. A month later, armed Germans and Ukrainians surrounded the wall as a Gestapo officer ordered all the Jews to assemble at the gate for deportation. What the Jews did then is told by Mendel Mann, who learned the story when he later reached the town with the Russian Army:

> Tuvia Tchubak . . . son of a blacksmith, and another Jew named Taflik began to exhort the people not to obey the German command but to gather in the synagogue instead. When the synagogue was filled, one Jew leaped to the platform and called out: "Resist! Do not go voluntarily like sheep!" Another jumped on a bench and cried out: "Jews! You should know that the pits have already been dug at the Katowice

forest!" The young people were in a fighting mood. One of them shouted: "Let's set the ghetto on fire! Burn it down! Burn everything!"

From somewhere barrels of kerosene were rolled out. Jews fetched ladles, pots, jugs, and other kitchen utensils and filled them with kerosene. Even children came running with pots. The few Orthodox Jews did not participate. They gathered in the large synagogue and read the Psalms.

When night fell, the Jews put the torch to the kerosene-soaked houses. Flames shot up in the air. Soon the whole ghetto was on fire. The Germans and Ukrainians, taken unaware, were stunned and confused, and the Jews turned the confusion into their advantage.

"Smash the fence!" someone cried out. The youths attacked the Germans and Ukrainians with hatchets. From some houses shots rang out and grenades were thrown. Jews stormed the wall and began to run in the direction of the forest, leaving behind them a burning ghetto. The flames were visible for miles around. . . . About 2,000 of the Jews reached the forest, though they fled under continuous German fire and were frequently attacked on the way by Ukrainians who lay in wait in their scattered huts.

By the fall of 1942, only 65,000 Jews were still alive in the Warsaw ghetto that had once held nearly half a million people. The ghetto was a tiny fragment of its old self, clumps of tenements surrounded by high fences of wood or barbed wire. Inside, a small number of left-wing Zionists and pioneer Zionist youths were planning resistance through the Jewish Fighting Organization (JFO) led by twenty-four-year-old Mordecai Anielewicz. Their few arms and explosives were either smuggled in or manufactured in crude workshops within the ghetto. In January 1943, Himmler visited Warsaw and ordered mass deportations to the death camps to resume. On January 18, the ghetto was surrounded, and 8,000 Jews were told to muster for deportation. Although taken by surprise, the ghetto fighters launched guerrilla attacks upon the Nazi forces. The Germans were astounded by the sudden and unexpected armed counterattack. A thousand Jews were killed within a few days, and 6,500 were taken off to death camps. But German losses were heavy, too. The JFO had proved the Nazi "supermen" were not invincible. And now the mass of Jews surviving in the ghetto gave active support to the Jewish boys and girls who had determined to meet the enemy with guns, even though it meant certain death.

The Nazis had to give up their plans for the peaceful, orderly obliteration of what had been the largest Jewish community in Europe. Over the next few months the smaller ghettos nearby were destroyed, as well as Cracow, one of the oldest Jewish communities in Poland. Meanwhile the JFO had grown to nearly 700 fighters, organized into 22 groups. The ghetto people had built bunkers for hiding and defense and had linked them with underground passages so that people could move from house to house and street to street. The fighters collected food, smuggled in or made more arms, and rid the ghetto of informers. Although an appeal for aid was rejected by the Poles outside, preparations for battle went on.

On April 19, German army, police, and SS units invaded in force—tanks, artillery, machine guns—under orders to crush the resistance and destroy the Warsaw ghetto. With revolvers, grenades, rifles, and bricks, the Jews fought back. They battled the Nazis on the streets and in the courtyards, from sewers and rooftops, showing a will to resist that electrified the world. The revolt lasted for weeks, enraging the Nazi leadership, who had thought their vastly superior numbers and firepower would eliminate the ghetto swiftly. In his diary for May 1, Goebbels noted "the exceedingly serious fighting in Warsaw between . . . our own Wehrmacht [armed forces] . . . and the rebellious Jews. . . . It shows what is to be expected of the Jews when they are in possession of arms. . . ."

After four weeks of continuous fighting, the ghetto had still not surrendered, although most of the revolt's leaders had been killed. On May 16, the German commander General Stroop claimed in his official report that the ghetto "no longer exists." The scattered remnants of Warsaw's Jews, hiding in the ruins, clashed here and there with Germans. Some of the fighters survived to take part in the Polish uprising more than a year later, in August 1944. To the Warsaw ghetto goes the honor of carrying out the first major civilian revolt against the Nazis in all of occupied Europe.

A month after the Warsaw Ghetto Uprising, the Jews of Bialystok defended themselves when Nazi troops began to liquidate their ghetto. Bialystok, a Polish city surrounded by immense forests, was a large textile center. When the Germans captured it in 1941, they massacred Jews by the thousands, day after day. Once they crammed several hundred into a synagogue and burned them alive. The murder stopped for a time when the Nazis decided to make use of the city's productive capacity. They pushed the Jews behind ghetto walls and forced them to labor. A resistance movement sprang up, with diverse political wings. One of them was the *Hehalutz*, a pioneer Zionist youth group led by Mordecai Tenenbaum. An extraordinary document exists, recording a debate in the Hehalutz executive committee over what resistance policy to follow. These excerpts show the tormenting decisions the young fighters faced:

MORDECAI: . . . *The few people sitting here are the last Halutzim in Poland. We are entirely surrounded by the dead. . . . We have to decide what to do tomorrow. . . . We can do two things: decide that with the first Jews to be deported now from Bialystok, we start our counterattack, that from tomorrow on nobody is allowed to hide during the action. Everybody will be mobilized. We can see to it that not one German leaves the ghetto alive, that not one factory is left standing. . . . Or we could decide to escape to the woods. . . . Each one of us will have to decide about his own life or death. But together we have to find a collective answer to the common question. . . .*

ISAAC: *What we're really debating is two different kinds of death. Attack means certain death. The other way means death two or three days later. . . .*

HERSHL: . . . *Only one thing remains for us: to organize collec-*

164

tive resistance in the ghetto, at any cost . . . to write a proud
chapter of Jewish Bialystok and our movement into history.
. . . Our duty is clear: with the first Jew to be deported, we
must begin our counteraction. If anyone succeeds in taking
arms from the murderer and going into the woods—fine. . . .
I have lost everything, all those near to me; still, there persists
the desire to live. But there is no choice. If I thought that not
only individuals could save themselves but 50 or 60 percent
of the ghetto Jews, I would say that our decision should be to
remain alive at any cost. But we are condemned to death.

SARAH: . . . It is better to remain living than to kill five Germans.
In a counteraction we will all die, without any possible doubt.
On the other hand, in the woods 40 or 50 percent of our people
can be saved. That will be our honor and that will be our history.
We are still needed; we shall yet be of use. . . .

ENOCH: No illusions! We have nothing to expect but liquidation
to the last Jew. We have a choice of two kinds of death. The
woods won't save us, and certainly rebellion in the ghetto won't.
There remains for us only to die honorably. . . . The woods
offer greater opportunities for revenge, but we must not go
there to live on the mercy of peasants, to buy our food and lives
for money. Going to the woods should mean to become active
partisans, but that requires arms. . . . If we do have enough
time left, we should acquire arms and go to the woods. But if
the Nazi action intervenes, we must answer as soon as they
touch the first Jew. . . .

ETHEL: Concretely—if an action is started in the next few days,
then our only choice can be a counteraction; but if we are
granted more time, we should work along the lines of taking to
the woods. I hope I can be equal to the duties that will be
imposed on us. It may be that in the course of events I shall
be strengthened. In any case, I am resolved to do everything
that needs to be done. . . . We are going to perform a
desperate act, whether we want to or not. Our fate is sealed, and
there remains for us only the choice between one kind of death
and another. I am calm.

Tenenbaum's own conviction prevailed: that the duty of the resistance was to fight inside the ghetto. In July 1943, the resistance groups finally achieved unity in the Anti-Fascist Fighting Bloc. Only a month later, the Nazis sent in troops to destroy the 40,000 Jews in the Bialystok ghetto. All the resistance had to fight with were twenty-five rifles, a hundred small arms, a few tommy guns, one machine gun, some hand grenades, and axes, scythes, knives, and bayonets. The Nazis drove the Jews into six narrow streets of the ghetto. The resistance forces tried to breach the ghetto wall so that everyone still alive could make for the forest to join up with the partisans. They failed. Miserably armed and with no room to maneuver, they had no chance against tanks and armored cars. "Even if we are too weak to defend our lives," said the resistance proclamation posted on the ghetto walls, "we are strong enough to defend our Jewish honor and human dignity, and thus prove to the world that we are captive but not defeated."

In four days of August 1943, the Jews of Bialystok were annihilated. And so it went—in Warsaw, Minsk, Slonim, Nieswiez, Czestochowa, Glebokie, Lachwa, Mazowiecki, Kleck, Breslau— Jews in the ghettos took up arms to resist their slaughter. Many Jews, like those of Tuczno, escaped to the forests or mountains and formed or joined partisan units. After Germany attacked Soviet Russia, guerrilla fighting increased. With Russia in the war, the Communists became much more active in the resistance movement throughout Europe. In Eastern Europe, when the Russian Army took the counteroffensive, the partisans often linked up with Russian-led guerrilla units.

The Jews who had survived the rebellion against the Nazis in Marcinkonis escaped to the forest. Their region, on the border between Lithuania and Byelorussia (in the western region of Soviet Russia), was a battleground for German army units and Russian partisans. The commander of the Russian partisans, a Jew named Davidov, befriended the Marcinkonis Jews, equipping them with weapons dropped by parachute. He forbade non-Jewish partisans to molest them. The Marcinkonis partisans, under their chief, Yitzhok Kobrovsky, plunged into guerrilla warfare. They derailed a military train and blew up a locomotive in their first action. Then they wrecked a dozen ammunition cars and ruined stretches of railway tracks. Their success led many other Jews hiding in the forests to join the partisans.

The Minsk ghetto supplied more Jews for the partisan movement than any other ghetto in Eastern Europe. Over 10,000 escaped into the forest with the help of the ghetto underground; they formed 7 partisan detachments. Some of them were mixed with non-Jewish Byelorussians, and the others were either all Jewish or mainly Jewish. One unit, headed by the underground leader Zorin, established a Family Camp of 600 men, women, and children. Its function was to supply the partisan units with boots and clothing and to operate a central laundry, bakery, and hospital for them. A combat section made up of the Family Camp's younger members protected the group and took part in the operations of other partisan units, too. Unlike the general population of Poland, the Byelorussians were friendly to Jews and made it possible for thousands to survive. The Jewish and Byelorussian undergrounds worked in close collaboration.

Another family unit of forest fighters was led by the three Bielski brothers of Byelorussia. It began in December 1941 when their parents were killed by the Germans. With 15 other Jews— friends and relatives from nearby villages—they formed a guerrilla unit armed with six rifles bought from a peasant. Their first action was to shoot a German guard and take his rifle and ammunition. That winter Jews streamed into their camp, and within a year the Bielski division of 500 fighters was ambushing German troops, dynamiting their trains, and wrecking their communications. The group gave protection to many old men and women and to children, although they hampered movement and drained food supplies. But noncombatants helped by cooking, building barracks, staffing the infirmary, and teaching the children. One of the major actions of the Bielskis was to wreck the granaries and burn the farms the Germans had taken over to support their armies. As the Wehrmacht retreated in the summer of 1944, the Bielski unit took part in the heavy fighting. Over 1,000 Jews in the family unit survived, thanks to the protection of the partisans.

Especially useful to the forest fighters were Jewish physicians and medical workers. One of the many who earned combat leadership was Dr. Ezekiel Atlas, a young Polish Jew educated as a physician in Western Europe. When the ghetto of Dereczyn was destroyed by the Nazis in July 1942, a handful of Jews escaped to the forest. Dr. Atlas molded a Jewish partisan unit out of them. To avenge the loss of their families, they attacked the German garrison in Dereczyn one night. After several hours of fighting, they captured 44 Germans, most of them police, and shot them in the same square where the Nazis had slaughtered Jews only three weeks earlier. This action, one of the first victories by a partisan unit, won wide recognition for the fighting talents of Jews. Atlas, whose parents and sister had been killed by the Nazis, would say to his partisans, "Our private lives finished on the day our fellow Jews were massacred. Every day of life that is given us belongs not to ourselves but to our slaughtered families. We must avenge them." A little man, Atlas looked funny wearing boots far too big for his small feet. He carried a submachine gun and a pistol, and the pockets of his ragged army pants bulged with hand grenades. He was enormously popular with his men. His unit destroyed bridges, blew up trains, and salvaged equipment and weapons abandoned by the German troops. In one attack on a German garrison, they killed 127 soldiers and captured 25 wagon-loads of weapons. Dr. Atlas' military career lasted less than six months. Only thirty-two, he was killed in December 1942 when Germans attacked his unit.

Just as heroic were the young men and women who acted as couriers between the partisans in the forests and the underground inside the ghettos. Zelda Tregar carried messages from partisan units into the Vilna ghetto, slipping through the barbed wire and past the sentries at least eighteen times. And from the ghetto she carried dozens of guns back to the guerrilla bases. She smuggled herself into several concentration camps and guided some of the prisoners to freedom. Four times she was captured by the Nazis, and four times she escaped from their hands.

Vitka Kempner had the same indomitable spirit. Like Zelda, she was one of the Vilna-ghetto fighters who fled to the forest to continue resistance. Once she hauled a suitcase packed with explosives into Vilna, a distance of 20 miles, and blew up an electric generator. Another time she slipped into the concentration camp at Kailis and led 60 prisoners to partisan camps. By herself she succeeded in capturing 2 Gestapo agents.

The core of partisan action was physical force. Any available weapon and any imaginable means were used to kill the Nazi enemy and thwart his murderous plans. The risks were enormous, and the casualties high. To die of a bullet was the easiest death to be faced. Many died gruesome and lingering deaths devised by experts in torture. And they died at the hands not only of Germans but of anti-Semitic and greedy Poles, Lithuanians, Hungarians, Rumanians, Letts, Estonians, Ukrainians . . . even other, native guerrilla bands. While fighting to destroy the Nazis, many of these peoples were just as hostile to the Jews, and freely plundered and butchered them.

This was the tragic case in Eastern Europe. It was not the same in Western Europe. The French historian of the Holocaust, Leon Poliakov, explains why:

> Great as was the tragedy of the Western Jews, it was not marked by the same brutality as in the East. The causes were various: on the one hand, the Jews in the West were more assimilated to their non-Jewish environment, they were few in number and were more widely distributed among the general population; on the other hand, the enemy pursued a different policy in the West than in the East. In the West he acted with greater cunning and circumspection, to avoid shocking the native population, which was not as contaminated with the germ of anti-Semitism as the peoples of Eastern Europe. The chief factor, however, was the attitude of the native population and the sympathy the Jews in the countries of the West received from their fellow citizens. The difference is most clearly revealed in the numerical comparison of the number of Jews who perished. In Poland more than 90 percent of the Jews were liquidated, in France . . . the losses were less than 30 percent.

In Nazi-occupied Paris there was a Jewish partisan unit which lived an altogether different life than the forest partisans of Eastern Europe. One of its leaders was Abraham Lissner, a veteran of the International Brigades who fought against Franco in Spain in the 1930s. In his diary he recorded what was required of a partisan in Paris:

1. *Sever relations with everyone who is not connected with the underground organization.*
2. *Abandon one's legal residence and begin living alone on an illegal basis.*

These strict measures had to be adopted so that the partisan, if arrested, would not drag others along with him. A partisan must spend his entire day outdoors even when he has no special reason for being on the street. To avoid arousing suspicion of his concierge and neighbors, he has to leave his room every morning at the same time, as though he were going to work, and return in the evening like all the other residents. Full-time partisans receive a monthly wage from the organization, since they have no other means of earning a living. A single partisan gets 1600 francs [$36.54] a month; a married one with one child gets 1900. On this salary the partisan must pay the rent for his room and eat every meal in a different restaurant.

Jewish women shared the danger equally with the men.

Like the men, they carry out sabotage acts, using time bombs and grenades. One day three of these women lost their lives in the course of carrying out their duty. As they came out of the Métro station Porte d'Orleans, they were caught in a police roundup, which is a daily occurrence in Paris. One of the women, Helen Kro, who was carrying the grenades, was the first to be caught. The police took her home, hoping to find there a weapons cache. While they were searching, Helen threw herself out of the window rather than fall into the hands of the Gestapo. She was killed instantly. The other two, who were also caught by the Vichy police, were later deported and were never heard from again.

Partisan plans could go terribly wrong, as Lissner's Paris diary showed:

April 1942: Our leadership decided that on May 1 the Jewish partisans should carry out an anti-German act of a military character by placing a time bomb close to a barracks occupied by German soldiers. Salek Bot, a young violinist, and Hersz Zimmerman, an engineer, undertook the difficult task of preparing the explosive.

April 27: Today the Jewish partisans suffered a severe loss. As our two comrades were putting together the bomb, in a small hotel room in the fifth arrondissement, something went wrong. The bomb exploded, killing Salek on the spot and critically wounding Hersz. But that was not all. After the explosion the police occupied the hotel room and succeeded in arresting 17 of our comrades who, not knowing about the accident, had come to see Salek and walked into a police trap.

But there were many successes, too.

November 10, 1942: Today Marcel Rayman and Nathan Lemberger placed a time bomb at the window of a hotel on Montmor, which is inhabited by high-ranking German officers, causing great damage.

November 15: A group of Jewish partisans, led by Mayer List, today placed two time bombs at the window of a German military barracks on rue de Vaugirard, killing several Hitlerites while they were eating breakfast. In this action two Jewish women participated. They carried the bombs.

November 26: Today the Jewish partisans have to their credit two anti-German acts. They bombed a hotel on rue St. Florine, and they placed two time bombs on a street not far from Place de la Concorde, where German soldiers usually pass in groups.

The bombs exploded just as the soldiers arrived, causing severe losses in their ranks. Both acts went through without a mishap.

Sometimes the Jewish partisans worked with others in joint actions. Germans holding key positions in occupied nations were the targets of assassination. Karl Ritter was the aide to Fritz Sauckel, the head of Hitler's compulsory-labor service. Ritter had deported hundreds of thousands of Frenchmen to Germany for slave labor. The partisan chiefs condemned him to death and assigned three men to carry out the sentence: a Spaniard; a German anti-Fascist; and Marcel Rayman, a young French Jew. The three waited for Ritter near his garage one September morning in 1943. As his car came out, the Spaniard fired at him. Ritter tried to leap out of his car, but Rayman shot him dead. Caught later and tortured for three months by the Gestapo, Rayman said to the Nazis: "I'm a Jew, and as a Jew I could not live without fighting against you." He was executed in February 1944.

Marching songs such as this were popular
among the young people's groups in the ghettos.
They were written to inspire purposeful
defiance of the Nazi war machine.

->>>

Nor, bruder, an anderer ritm
Vet bald tsu dayn oyer dergeyn,
Un di, vos far shrek
Geven ersht farshtekt,
Shpanen mit undz nit aleyn.
Tsu eyns, tsvey, dray,
Tsu eyns, tsvey, dray,
Di geslech, dem toyer farlozt!
S'hot der trot aza klang
Gor anander gezang,
Ven du geyst un du veyst shoyn farvos.

But, brother, another rhythm
Will soon reach your ear,
And those who were hidden
In fear only yesterday,
Now march right along with us, not alone.
And one, two, three,
And one, two, three,
Leave the lanes and the gates behind!
For your step now resounds
With a new kind of sound,
When you march and know the reason why.

17

Revolt in the Death Camps

Even in the death camps there were bloody uprisings against the fate Hitler had decreed. That there could be any resistance within the camps seems almost impossible. The divisions among the prisoners were many: a score of different languages; a whole range of political beliefs; varying religious faiths; differences in class origin, in education, and in occupation or profession. These differences the SS were always ready to intensify in order to keep the inmates disunited.

And what time was there to think or plot, when the tiny spark of energy or spirit that might still live within a prisoner went into finding the extra morsel of food to stay alive or to stave off the next blow from a brutal kapo? To plan resistance, conspirators need to be able to meet and talk. But these prisoners were never alone. They slept, ate, washed, toileted, and worked, always under watchful eyes and listening ears. Cut off from the world outside, pitted against one another, it was natural to sink into hopelessness.

How could resistance be organized under such conditions? Yet it was. Small, inadequate, but it did appear. Shaye Gertner, who was fourteen when he was deported from Lodz to a camp, told how even in Dachau a group of prisoners practiced sabotage. He was one of the slave laborers in a munitions plant dug into the earth below Dachau. They made a weapon called "Fau 1."

*We not only produced bombs but manufactured the entire
apparatus, including five bombs and a bombing vessel. . . .
Former Soviet officers working with us taught us the art of
sabotage. They taught us to drop a few straws into receptacles
filled with gasoline. When the mechanism would be heated, the
straws would ignite and cause havoc. We also mixed sand with
the powder. The sabotage was not carried out carefully, and one
day all the apparatus was destroyed in the same manner. A
military commission investigating the explosion found sand and
straw. A rollcall of those employed in the tunnel followed,
separating the Jews, the Poles and the Russians. Every tenth
man was condemned to death—160 deaths all told. Thereafter,
the supervisor was most rigorous. At the least suspicion 30
to 50 workers would be hanged. Later we resumed the sabotage
so that the two or three parts of the apparatus would be de-
fective.*

In Treblinka, a young Jew from Warsaw, who worked in one of
the companies handling disposal of the victims, saw his wife and
child being taken to the gas chamber. He pulled out a concealed
knife and stabbed the SS guard to death. The same desire for
revenge burned in most hearts, but only in some did it develop
into a plan for revolt. In Treblinka, the revolutionary was a fifty-
year-old doctor from Warsaw named Julian Chorazyski. He
gathered a small group of plotters, among them Stanislaw Kohn.
They figured out a way to get dynamite and arms, but before they
could move ahead, the doctor was caught and took poison. His
place was taken by Galewski, an engineer from Lodz, and a Jewish
army officer from Czechoslovakia, Captain Zielo.

When the last transport of Jews from Warsaw brought in news
of the ghetto revolt, the conspirators decided this was the time for
their uprising. But months dragged on before they were ready.
And day after day they watched thousands of Jews, stripped
naked, lining up before the building which contained the twelve
gas chambers. Finally the conspirators fixed the time to act:
Monday, August 2, 1943, at 5 P.M. The plan was to ambush and

kill the chief murderers, disarm the guards, cut the telephone wires, and then destroy the killing center by fire. They would do this by filling a disinfectant sprinkler with gasoline stolen from camp trucks, spraying the gas over all the buildings they could, and then, at a given signal, hurling hand grenades at the "disinfected" sites to set them on fire. After this, they would free the Poles from a camp a mile away, join up with them, and escape to the woods to organize a partisan band. Only the 60 people who planned the revolt knew its details. As Stanislaw Kohn told:

> At two in the afternoon the distribution of weapons began. Young Salzberg and the other boys searched their employers' huts for weapons and took them to the garage. . . . The door of the armory was opened with our key and Jacek, the Hungarian boy, slipped inside, climbed onto the windowsill at the end of the room, cut out a small square in the glass with a diamond and handed out the bombs and other weapons to Jacob Miller . . . who put them on his refuse cart. The arms were carried to the garage. . . .
>
> Spirits grew agitated and no one could keep the secret. The leaders therefore decided to start the revolt an hour before the agreed time. Punctually at four the messages were sent to all groups with orders to assemble immediately in the garage to get their weapons. Rudek from Plotzk was responsible for the distribution.
>
> Anyone coming to fetch weapons had to give the password, "Death," to which the reply was "Life!" "Death—Life!" "Death—Life!" Cries of enthusiasm arose as the long-hoped-for guns, revolvers and hand grenades were distributed. At the same time the chief murderers of the camp were attacked. Telephonic communication was cut and the watchtowers were set on fire with gasoline. Captain Zielo attacked two SS guards with an ax and made his way to us to take over the command.
>
> Near the garage stood a German armored car, but Rudek had swiftly immobilized the engine. Now the car served as a lair from which to fire on the Germans. Our gunfire felled the

Sturmführer *Kurt Majdkur and other German dogs. The armory was taken by assault and the weapons distributed. We already had 200 armed men. The others attacked the Germans with axes and spades.*

We set fire to the gas chambers, burned the fake railway stations with all the notices . . . burned the barracks. . . .

The flames and the reports of the firing roused the Germans, who began to arrive from all sides. SS and police arrived from Kosow, soldiers from the nearby airfield and finally a special section of the Warsaw SS. Orders had been given to make for the neighboring forest. Most of our fighters fell but there were many German casualties. Very few of us survived.

Of the 700 prisoners drawn into the action, about 150 to 200 managed to escape. And of these, only a dozen lived through the war. More than 20 Germans were killed in the revolt. But the number who survived or the number who died is not a measure of the revolt's success. The Treblinka resistance had known they could get no support from the outside. Their goal had been to destroy the killing center. As Samuel Rajzman, one of the few survivors, said later, "We realized our aim fully and in martyrdom. Treblinka was wiped out. A fortress of horrible Nazism was erased from the face of the earth."

Scarcely two months later, another revolt occurred in the death camp of Sobibor. Here is the terse report of it made by the Order Police in the district of Lublin on the next day, October 15:

On October 14, 1943, at about 5 P.M., revolt of the Jews in SS-camp Sobibor, 25 miles north of Chelm. They overpowered the guards, seized the armory, and after firefight with camp garrison, fled in unknown direction. Nine SS murdered, 1 SS man missing, 2 foreign guards shot to death.

Approximately 300 Jews escaped; the remainder were shot to death or are now in camp. Military police and armed forces were notified immediately. The area south and southwest of Sobibor is now being searched by police and armed forces.

The uprising was all the more extraordinary because it came out of an underground movement that originated only three weeks before the attack. Its leader was Alexander Pechersky, a Jew and a Russian Army officer captured by the Germans. He directed about 70 other Jewish prisoners of war. Those who escaped split up. The Polish Jews went west, toward Chelmno, where they knew the language and the people. The Soviet Jews headed east. The Dutch, French, and German Jews knew not where to turn in this strange land. Half the escapees were killed quickly—by land mines, SS, police, troops, pursuing planes, and anti-Semitic Poles. The group that followed Pechersky, some 60 men and women, reached safety in a Russian partisan camp. Research indicates that 10 SS men and 38 Ukrainian guards were killed.

Two days after the uprising, Himmler ordered Sobibor to be totally destroyed. The revolt had succeeded in eliminating a death factory which had taken the lives of 600,000 Jews.

One year later, and another revolt in a death camp. This time at the largest—Auschwitz. It happened not long after the Nazi killers recorded the highest number of victims to be destroyed in one day: on July 24, 1944, they gassed and burned 46,000 Jews at Auschwitz.

The Russian armies were taking Poland from the Nazis. Soon they would reach the death camps. The Germans wavered over whether to blow up the crematoriums or to keep their fires burning. They decided to speed up the death machine.

For months the underground in Auschwitz had been trying to reach the outside world with convincing proof of Hitler's stepped-up exterminations. Their hope was to break through the universal indifference toward the condemned Jews. The reports which had already been sent abroad had not convinced any of the Allied governments to act. The underground decided that only the personal testimony of prisoners would achieve their aim.

But how get a prisoner out of Auschwitz? Its combined labor and death camps were encircled by electrified barbed wire, deep ditches, high watchtowers. Guards and informers were everywhere. For 40 kilometers around, the territory had been declared "prohibited" and cleared of all civilians. Still, prisoners did escape. At least 230 attempts have been recorded; about 80 succeeded. Of these, five were not personal flights but escapes of Jewish prisoners organized by the underground to tell the world what was happening inside the death factory. The five were Siegfried Lederer, Walter Rosenberg, Alfred Wetzler, Arnost Rosin, and Czezlaw Mordowicz. The first man escaped on April 5, 1944; the next two on April 7; and the last two on May 27. Their detailed eyewitness testimonies, given to both private and governmental agencies, were accompanied by concrete proposals that the Allied governments should bomb from the air the gas chambers, the crematoriums, the industrial plants, and the railway lines used for the daily transports. They urged that public threats of retaliation be given repeatedly over the radio, and they asked that the Vatican issue a strong condemnation of the Nazi crimes. The hope was to prevent the final stage of the extermination process being prepared by the Nazis for the spring of 1944.

But what was done? Only verbal protests were made. Nothing practical was attempted in answer to the appeals. The reply of the United States government, for instance, was that the planes for bombing raids on the camps could not be spared in the midst of war. "Such an effort, even if practicable, might provoke even more vindictive [acts] by the Germans," said John J. McCloy, the U.S. Assistant Secretary of War.

The only thing left for the prisoners to do was to try to destroy Auschwitz by themselves.

One day Rosa Robota, a twenty-three-year-old Jewish prisoner (from the Polish town of Ciechanow) who worked in the clothing-supply section of Auschwitz, was approached by a stranger. Rosa was a member of *Hashomer Hatzair*, the Socialist-Zionist youth movement which prepared people for kibbutz life in Palestine. The stranger was Noah Zabladowicz, a member of the Jewish underground in the camp. He told her the organization was planning a general uprising during which they wanted to blow up the gas chambers and crematoriums. They needed explosives to do it. Since she had friends from her hometown who worked in the explosives section of the Krupp munitions plant at Auschwitz, would she try to get those young women to help?

Rosa was eager to carry out the task. Her own family, together with almost all the other Jews of Ciechanow, had been sent to the gas chamber. She hated the Nazis. She soon had 20 young women smuggling dynamite and explosive charges out of the plant. They hid the tiny dynamite wheels in their bras or in secret pockets of their clothing. The material was made into bombs by a Russian prisoner who used empty sardine tins for casings. The bombs were then hidden in various parts of the huge camp. One cache was hidden by the Sonderkommando who lived next to the crematoriums where they worked. The Sonderkommando was the group of Jewish prisoners assigned by the SS to spend the last few months of their lives operating the crematoriums. Each group was then itself gassed and replaced by another crew. Rosa brought the bombs to the Sonderkommando, who hid them in the handcarts in which the corpses of prisoners who had died in the barracks were taken to the crematoriums.

Before the uprising could take place, the Sonderkommando learned that their turn to be gassed was imminent. They had no choice but to act now or go to their deaths passively. They blew up Crematorium Number 3, killing 4 SS men and wounding others. Then they broke through the barbed wire and fled. About 600 prisoners got loose in the uproar, but the Nazis hunted them down and killed them.

With the help of informers, the SS traced the trail of the explosives to the young women in the munitions plant. Three who worked there—Esther, Ella, and Regina (their full names are unknown)—together with Rosa Robota, were seized for grilling. Fearing Rosa would not be able to withstand the terrible torture, the underground found a way to get her friend Noah in to see her. The Jewish kapo let him into her cell, and then left them alone briefly. Noah reported later:

When I became accustomed to the dark, I noticed a figure wrapped in torn clothing, lying on the cold cement floor. She turned her head toward me and I hardly recognized her. After several minutes of silence she began to speak. She told me of the sadistic methods the Germans employed during interrogations. It is impossible for a human being to endure them. She told me that she took all the blame upon herself and that she would be the last to go. She had betrayed no one.

I tried to console her but she would not listen. I know what I have done, and what I am to expect, she said. She asked that the comrades continue with their work. It is easier to die when one knows that the work is being carried on.

I heard the door squeak. Jacob ordered me to come out. We took leave of each other. It was the last time that I saw her.

Rosa gave Noah a last message for the underground. It ended with the Hebrew greeting of the Hashomer Hatzair: "Khazak v' hamatz"—Be strong and brave.

Soon after, all the Jewish prisoners in the camp were marched to the execution site. They stood at the foot of the gallows and watched as Rosa and her three comrades died. Auschwitz had not broken them. While they lived, they fought back.

18

The Only Hope Left

Russian troops advanced into Poland, freeing prisoners in the Maidanek death camp in July 1944. Even as the Germans, knowing they had lost the war, retreated, they saw to it that half a million Hungarian Jews were gassed in day-and-night operations in Auschwitz. Not until the end of November did that death machine halt. The SS blew up the crematoriums, destroyed the camp records, and burned the vast storehouses of looted property. To prevent the liberation of survivors in the other camps of Poland and the Baltic region, the SS pushed them west, back toward Germany, throughout the bitter winter months. They dumped the prisoners inside Germany, where Hitler was making his last stand. Given no food, ravaged by typhus, the human wrecks died by the tens of thousands. Just as freedom came in sight . . .

In the last days of the war, the Nazi leaders holed up in Hitler's concrete bunker beneath the debris of bombed Berlin. A week before Germany surrendered, Hitler committed suicide. In his final testament he continued to vilify the Jews, "the universal poisoner of all nations." They had caused the war, not he. He charged the new leaders of Germany to "uphold the racial laws."

A few weeks before the war's end, seventeen-year-old Elie Wiesel was one of the 20,000 prisoners still alive in Buchenwald. The SS decided to evacuate them all before the American troops could reach them. As they began taking their last victims to the assembly point, shots rang out and grenades exploded all over the camp. The resistance had chosen this moment to revolt. The SS fled; the underground was in charge. Wiesel describes the moment:

> At about six o'clock in the evening, the first American tank stood at the gates of Buchenwald.
>
> Our first act as free men was to throw ourselves onto the provisions. We thought only of that. Not of revenge, not of our families. Nothing but bread.
>
> And even when we were no longer hungry, there was still no one who thought of revenge. On the following day, some of the young men went to Weimar to get some potatoes and clothes—and to sleep with girls. But of revenge, not a sign.
>
> Three days after the liberation of Buchenwald I became very ill with food poisoning. I was transferred to the hospital and spent two weeks between life and death.
>
> One day I was able to get up, after gathering all my strength. I wanted to see myself in the mirror hanging on the opposite wall. I had not seen myself since the ghetto.
>
> From the depths of the mirror, a corpse gazed back at me.
>
> The look in his eyes, as they stared into mine, has never left me.

Twenty months after he had been taken prisoner in Italy and deported to Auschwitz, Primo Levi came home.

> Of 650, our number when we had left, three of us were returning. . . . My house was still standing, all my family was alive, no one was expecting me. I was swollen, bearded, and in rags, and had difficulty in making myself recognized. I found my friends full of life, the warmth of secure meals, the solidity of daily work, the liberating joy of recounting my story. I found a large clean bed, which in the evening (a moment of terror) yielded softly under my weight. But only after many months did I lose the habit of walking with my glance fixed to the ground, as if searching for something to eat or to pocket hastily to sell

183

for bread; and a dream full of horror has still not ceased to visit me, at sometimes frequent, sometimes longer, intervals.

It is a dream within a dream, varied in detail, one in substance. I am sitting at a table with my family, or with friends, or at work or in the green countryside; in short, in a peaceful relaxed environment, apparently without tension or affliction; yet I feel a deep and subtle anguish, the definite sensation of an impending threat. And in fact, as the dream proceeds, slowly or brutally, each time in a different way, everything collapses and disintegrates around me, the scenery, the wall, the people, while the anguish becomes more intense and more precise. Now everything has changed to chaos; I am alone in the center of a grey and turbid nothing, and now, I know what this thing means, and I also know that I have always known it; I am in the Lager once more, and nothing is true outside the Lager. All the rest was a brief pause, a deception of the senses, a dream; my family, nature in flower, my home. Now this inner dream, this dream of peace, is over, and in the outer dream, which continues, gelid, a well-known voice resounds: a single word, not imperious, but brief and subdued. It is the dawn command of Auschwitz, a foreign word, feared and expected: Get up, 'Wstawàch!

What of the future? Was there any hope for the Jews of Europe, the remnant, the one out of three, still alive? As Primo Levi was journeying home from Auschwitz to Italy, his train passed through Germany, and he caught a glimpse of the future.

After Munich we realized that we had taken on board an entire contingent: our train consisted no longer of 60, but of 61 cars. A new car was traveling with us towards Italy at the end of our train, crammed with young Jews, boys and girls, coming from all the countries of Eastern Europe. None of them seemed more than twenty years old, but they were extremely self-confident and resolute people; they were young Zionists, on their way to Israel, traveling where they were able to, and finding a path where they could. A ship was waiting for them at

Bari; they had purchased their car, and it had proved the
simplest thing in the world to attach it to our train: they had not
asked anybody's permission, but had hooked it on, and that
was that. I was amazed, but they laughed at my amazement:
"Hitler's dead, isn't he?" replied their leader, with his intense
hawklike glance. They felt immensely free and strong, lords
of the world and of their destinies.

Many East European Jews who outlived Hitler felt they could
no longer stay in their homeland. One of them was Tuviah Friedman, who later became known as a hunter of Nazi criminals.
Poland after the war only tolerated the Jews, while pretending
that anti-Semitism no longer existed. Friedman decided to leave
for Palestine, to join with Jews from all over the world in the fight
for a national home. Early one morning in the spring of 1946,
together with a group of others, he climbed down a mountain and
crossed the Polish border into Czechoslovakia.

I looked behind me, at Poland. My father and his father were
buried there. Jews had lived in Poland for a thousand years,
their condition fluctuating like the fever of a malaria patient.
One hour back, I thought, is the country in which I was born,
to which I had shown allegiance, which I had tried to love;
now, here, with a packful of clothing, happy that I had succeeded in crossing its frontier, I sat catching my breath, gather-
ing up my strength for an unknown future. I had perhaps a
total of ten dollars, and some socks and shirts and underclothing.
Everything else was in my heart.

A few months later Poland proved how right Tuviah Friedman
had been. A pogrom erupted in Kielce on July 4, 1946. A mob
stormed the Jewish community center and murdered 41 Jews. Like
a string of bombs, pogroms exploded all over the country.

After the great hour of liberation, many of the ex-prisoners
suffered intense attacks of depression. They were no longer
Untermenschen, but did going on with life make any sense? No
one was left to live for. There was no home to return to.

Then they began to think, Maybe somebody else is alive. Wife, husband, parents, children, friends, people in the hometown? Simon Wiesenthal saw the day he had prayed for all those years— the day the last SS man ran away, as American tanks rumbled into the Mauthausen camp. But he didn't believe in miracles. He knew all of his people were dead. His wife—buried in the rubble of Warsaw. His mother—dead in the death camp of Belzec. Still, he wrote the Red Cross in Geneva; they replied that his wife was dead. He watched the other survivors begin their hunt.

There was no mail service. The few available telephone lines were restricted to military use. The only way to find out whether someone was alive was to go and look. Across Europe a wild tide of frantic survivors was flowing. People were hitch-hiking, getting short jeep rides, or hanging on to dilapidated railway coaches without windows or doors. They sat in huddled groups on hay carts, and some just walked. They would use any means to get a few miles closer to their destination. To get from Linz to Munich, normally a three-hour railroad trip, might take five days. Many of them didn't really know where to go. To the place where one had been with his family before the war? To the concentration camp where the family had last been heard of? Families had been torn apart too suddenly to make arrangements for the day when it would be all over.

. . . And yet the survivors continued their pilgrimage of despair, sleeping on highways or in railroad stations, waiting for another train, another horse-drawn cart to come along, always driven to hope. "Perhaps someone is still alive. . . ." Someone might tell where to find a wife, a mother, children, a brother— or whether they were dead. Better to know the truth than to know nothing. The desire to find one's people was stronger than hunger, thirst, fatigue. Stronger even than the fear of border patrols . . . of men saying, "Let's see your papers."

And then the miracle: his wife had survived. They found each other six months after the war ended.

The Wiesenthals, husband and wife, were among the lucky

ones. Hitler's Final Solution had not destroyed all of Europe's Jews. Not quite all. One out of ten of Poland's prewar Jewish community of 3.3 million was still alive in 1945. But for most of those who had escaped the gas chambers, this place could no longer be home. Even when governments changed, Jews saw that they could still be victims. Through all of Poland's shifts—from czarist province to independent republic and now to postwar Communist state—there was one constant: anti-Semitism.

Palestine was the only hope left. Governments throughout the world had refused to take Jews in when they were trying to flee Hitler. None offered to take in the remnant now. The illegal entry to Palestine, which had begun when Britain curbed immigration in 1939, continued after the war. By 1947, 113,000 Jewish refugees had slipped through the barriers. The violent struggle for Palestine among Jews, Arabs, and the British went to the United Nations for solution. The United Nations agreed on a partition plan for separate Jewish and Arab states in Palestine. The Jews accepted the proposal; the Arabs refused it. The British departed, and the independent state of Israel was proclaimed on May 14, 1948.

The immediate consequence was the invasion of Israel by seven Arab states. A UN truce ended the war, leaving Israel with more territory than the UN Partition Plan had allotted it. The new state opened its doors to the ingathering of exiles. Thousands of Jewish settlers from all over the world, aided by the Joint Distribution Committee, made their way to Israel. (One out of every seven Israelis in those early years came out of a concentration camp. One out of every three Israelis had lost one or more relatives to Hitler's extermination machine.) By 1975 Israel's Jewish population stood at 2.6 million.

The hope of finding common ground between Arabs and Jews is still alive, although challenges from the Arab world resulted in the two wars of 1967 and 1973. To Jews everywhere, Israel was defending the right of the Jewish people to exist. It was a right Jews had to secure for themselves. They could count on no one else. Thousands of years of bitter experience had taught them that as long as Jews were a minority, they would always be persecuted. The Holocaust had signified their near-destruction. It had happened once; it could happen again.

And the rest of the world? It did little about the Jews during the war, and not much more after it.

What about the perpetrators of the crime? The four leading Allied powers—the United States, the Soviet Union, Britain, and France—debated what to do about them. Finally it was agreed to try the instigators of the war for their "crimes against humanity." The chief charge was that of aggressive war. In preparing for the Nuremberg Trials of 1945 and carrying them out, the prosecutors gave evidence demonstrating that the Germans had committed enormous crimes against humanity. Robert H. Jackson, the U.S. Chief Prosecutor at Nuremberg, said the world had never "witnessed slaughter on such a scale, such cruelties and inhumanities, such wholesale deportations of people into slavery, such annihilations of minorities. . . . If we cannot eliminate the causes and prevent the repetition of these barbaric events, it is not an irresponsible prophecy to say that the twentieth century may yet succeed in bringing the doom of civilization."

The first trial began late in 1945 before an international military tribunal. The 22 men in the dock had held key positions in the Nazi machinery of destruction. Now they claimed ignorance. They "did not know," they said, that the Jews were to be exterminated. Even so, they protested that whatever they did, they did under orders. From whom? From Adolf Hitler, of course.

When this trial ended in October 1946, 12 of the defendants were sentenced to death, 3 to life imprisonment, 4 to lesser terms, and 3 were acquitted. There was no popular movement to launch mass trials of the huge number of Germans who were part of the death machine. Not even among the Jews. The trials of "lesser offenders" that followed were the result of a tangled elimination process, chiefly in the American and British zones of occupied Germany. Less than 200 men all told were brought into court in the American zone. They included generals, judges, industrialists, physicians, concentration-camp administrators, and leaders of the mobile killing squads. After judgment, great reductions of sentence were often given by the U.S. High Commissioner to Germany and his clemency board.

The Germans themselves did little to punish their own war criminals. The small number convicted in German courts got unbelievably easy sentences, and they and the great number who were exonerated went back to their everyday lives, shrugging off the past. Many retired with pensions. Some entered politics, rising to high office. There were many notorious Nazis who disappeared immediately after the war, finding refuge in Spain, Latin America, the Middle East, and the United States. (Adolf Eichmann was one of those discovered in hiding and tried in 1961 for his crimes.)

Later, the West German government offered "amends" to the Jews. Three measures were adopted: restitution, reparations, and indemnification. These provided benefits only to the surviving victims; nothing was done to compensate for the 6 million dead.

Restitution meant the return of identifiable property to the original owner or payment for it if he did not wish to take it back. The total amounted to several hundred million dollars. Reparations were paid as the result of a treaty made in 1952 between West Germany and Israel. Israel received some $700 million in commodity shipments; and survivors in other countries, about another $100 million. Through the indemnification program, West Germany paid for various kinds and degrees of losses suffered as the direct or indirect result of official German action. The full benefits went only to victims who had resided on German soil at some time.

THE DEATH TOLL

Country*	Jewish population, September 1939	Number of Jews dead	Percentage of Jews dead
Poland	3,300,000	2,800,000	85.0
Soviet Union (occupied area)	2,100,000	1,500,000	71.4
Rumania	850,000	425,000	50.0
Hungary	404,000	200,000	49.5
Czechoslovakia	315,000	260,000	82.5
France**	300,000	90,000	30.0
Germany	210,000	170,000	81.0
Lithuania	150,000	135,000	90.0
Holland**	150,000	90,000	60.0
Latvia	95,000	85,000	89.5
Belgium**	90,000	40,000	44.4
Greece	75,000	60,000	80.0
Yugoslavia	75,000	55,000	73.3
Austria	60,000	40,000	66.6
Italy**	57,000	15,000	26.3
Bulgaria	50,000	7,000	14.0
Miscellaneous#	20,000	6,000	30.0
Totals	8,301,000	5,978,000	72.0

* Considered within prewar borders
** Figures include Jewish refugees
\# Denmark, Estonia, Luxembourg, Norway, and the city of Danzig, Poland

(Source: Hannah Vogt, THE BURDEN OF GUILT)

190

Never to Forget

This, then, is not the Holocaust—what words can be equal to it?—but merely something about it. We who did not live it can know at least this much.

To forget what we know would not be human.

To remember it is to think of what being human means. The Holocaust was a measure of man's dimensions. One can think of the power of evil it demonstrated—and of those people who treated others as less than human, as bacteria. Or of the power of good—and of those people who held out a hand to others.

By nature, man is neither good nor evil. He has both possibilities. And the freedom to realize the one or the other. "The power of choosing between good and evil," said the early Christian philosopher Origen, "is within the reach of all."

There are forces at work in the world which cut off human response. They make it possible for people to commit terrible crimes without knowing or feeling they are doing wrong. Eichmann was one such person. He saw himself as only a tiny cog in the machine destroying inhuman objects, the Jews. He was "doing his duty." He was the product of a totalitarian state. Such systems deform and depersonalize those they rule. Whether of the right or the left, they make functionaries out of us, mere nobodies reduced to so much machinery.

Thus it is that the massacre of a whole people can be organized and carried out by the State, relying upon this "human" ma-

191

chinery. The individual conscience vanishes in the face of "orders from superiors." Only a few people in Germany still made their own judgments of right or wrong, and acted accordingly. They did not let the State decide for them; they took personal responsibility in questions of morality. Even under the worst conditions of terror some people will resist evil.

If there had been more people like that—not only in Germany but everywhere—the Holocaust might not have happened. Before the war started, there were many chances to save the Jews. The world was indifferent. After the war began, there were still ways to save some. The will to do it was not there. The conscience of man, the sympathy of one human being for another, failed. Perhaps, it could be argued, by that time it was too late. But who even tried hard enough?

If few did, then it is hard to believe that the shock of Auschwitz makes impossible another Holocaust. Emil Fackenheim, the philosopher and a survivor of the Holocaust, asks: "Is the grim truth not rather that a second Holocaust has been made more likely, not less likely, by the fact of the first? For there are few signs anywhere of that radical repentance which alone could rid the world of Hitler's shadow."

In Indochina, in Indonesia, in Biafra, in Bangladesh, there have been mass exterminations: all post-Hitler. Who speaks of them now? Hitler himself, contemplating the extermination of the Jews, said, Who remembers that the Turks massacred a million Armenians only a little while ago?

Indifference is the greatest sin.

It can become as powerful as an action. Not to do something against evil is to participate in the evil. Karl Jaspers, the German philosopher, wrote shortly after the Holocaust that every German was to be blamed for "crimes committed in his presence or with his knowledge. If I fail to do whatever I can to prevent them, I too am guilty. If I was present at the murder of others without risking my life to prevent it, I feel guilty."

From Alexander Donat, a survivor of the Warsaw ghetto, there is this last word:

The shame and horror of our century have to do with the conduct of the European powers, the Gentile world. Even if not one Jew had resisted, there would be no justification either to condemn the victims or to divert attention from the crimes of the murderers. The central issue must not be forgotten: it is a moral issue, the issue of what the world has done and permitted to be done. To insist upon making the world uncomfortable with the memory of its guilt is a necessity for that moral reconstruction which may alone prevent a repetition of our Holocaust.

CHRONOLOGY

1933

Jan.	30	Germany's President Hindenburg appoints Adolf Hitler, head of the Nazi party, as Reich Chancellor (Prime Minister).
Feb.	2	Political demonstrations are banned in Germany.
	27–28	Reichstag fire. State of emergency declared. Constitutional rights suspended.
Mar.	5	Last general election to Reichstag: Nazis receive 44% of vote. First "individual acts" against Jewish citizens.
	23	First concentration camps: Dachau opens.
Apr.	1	First official boycott of Jewish shops and businesses throughout Germany.
July	14	Nazi party made Germany's one and only legal party. Political opposition punishable by law. Jews deprived of German citizenship.
Dec.	1	Hitler declares German state and Nazi party are one by law.

1934

Jan.	2	Laws for sterilization of "unfit."
Aug.	2	On death of Hindenburg, Hitler becomes Germany's Head of State and Commander-in-Chief of Armed Forces.

1935

Sept.	15	Reichstag passes anti-Semitic Nuremberg Laws: the "Reich Citizenship Law" defines "Jews" and "mixed-blood" status, and the "Law for the Protection of

German Blood and German Honor" prohibits marriage between Jews and Aryans.

1936

Mar.	7	German troops occupy the Rhineland, violating the Versailles treaty.
Oct.	25	Hitler and Mussolini form Rome-Berlin Axis for war.
Nov.	25	Germany and Japan sign military pact.

1937

July	16	Buchenwald concentration camp opens.
Nov.	5	Hitler discloses war plans at secret meeting.

1938

Mar.	13	German army takes over Austria and applies anti-Jewish laws.
Apr.	22	Decree issued to eliminate Jews from Germany's economy and to take over their assets.
June	15	Arrests begin of all "previously convicted Jews," including those convicted of such minor offenses as traffic violations.
July	6	At international conference at Evian, France, participating nations fail to provide refuge for German Jews.
Sept.	29	In Munich pact, Britain and France agree to allow Hitler's annexation of Czech Sudetenland.
Oct.	5	Passports of German Jews marked with letter "J."
	28	Thousands of Jews in Germany expelled into Poland.
Nov.	7	Herschel Grynszpan shoots member of German embassy staff in Paris, resulting in:
	9	"Night of Broken Glass" (*Kristallnacht*), in which government organizes pogroms against Jews throughout Germany.
	12	At Nazi conference on "Jewish problem," Goering orders "expiation payment" by Jews and their exclusion from economic and cultural life. About 26,000 Jews arrested and sent to concentration camps; 1,000 killed.
	15	Jewish children expelled from German schools.
Dec.		Decree orders "Aryanization" (compulsory expropria-

tion) of Jewish shops, industries, and businesses throughout Germany.

1939

Jan.	1	German Jews compelled to use first name of "Sarah" or "Israel."
	30	In Reichstag speech, Hitler prophesies "the extermination of the Jewish race in Europe" in case of war.
Mar.	15	German troops occupy Czechoslovakia, without opposition from other nations.
Aug.	23	Germany and Soviet Union sign non-aggression pact.
Sept.	1	Germany invades Poland: World War II begins. SS and German army cooperate in widespread pogroms and mass executions in Poland.
	3	Great Britain and France declare war on Germany.
	27	Poland surrenders to Germany. Forced labor announced for Polish Jews.
Oct.	12	Nazis begin deporting Jews from Austria and Moravia to Poland.
Nov.		Hans Frank made Governor General of occupied Poland: establishes first Polish ghetto; begins to set up a Jewish Council (*Judenrat*) in each city.

1940

Jan.		First resistance actions by Jewish youth in Poland.
Apr.	9	German invasion of Denmark and Norway.
May	10–18	German invasion of Holland, Belgium, Luxembourg, France. Holland surrenders. Belgium surrenders. Auschwitz concentration camp (later to become a death camp) opens.
June	10–22	Italy enters war as Hitler's ally. France surrenders.
Sept.	27	Japan joins Germany and Italy to form Axis Powers. Soon Hungary, Rumania, and Slovakia join Axis.
Nov.	15	Warsaw ghetto sealed off.
Dec.		Emmanuel Ringelblum begins work on secret archives of Jewish life in Warsaw ghetto.

1941

Feb.	22	Deportation of Dutch Jews to Mauthausen concentration camp begins; Holland's workers strike in sympathy with Jews.

June	22	Hitler breaks non-aggression pact with Stalin; invades Soviet Union. Nazi massacres begin in Eastern Europe.
July	12	Britain and Soviet Union sign military treaty to co-operate against Hitler.
	31	Goering appoints Heydrich to carry out "Final Solution of the Jewish Question."
Sept.	1	Jewish star introduced: all German Jews (ages six up) must wear it, beginning September 19.
Oct.	14	German Jews deported to Lodz, Poland (beginning of general deportations from Reich).
Dec.	7	Japanese attack Pearl Harbor. U.S. joins Allied Powers (Britain and USSR) in war against Axis Powers.
	8	Chelmno death camp begins functioning. Jewish partisans begin operating in Minsk area.

1942

Jan.	15	Nazis begin transporting Jews from Lodz to Chelmno death camp.
	20	Wannsee conference on Nazi plan to exterminate European Jews.
	21	Unified Partisan Organization set up in Vilna ghetto. Jewish resistance groups grow throughout Eastern Europe.
April		Transports from ghettos to death camps extend over Poland.
June	1	Treblinka death camp opens. Jewish star introduced in Nazi-occupied France and Holland.
July	22	Jews offer armed resistance during liquidation of Nieswiez ghetto. Similar actions follow in other ghettos.
	28	Jewish Fighting Organization (JFO) set up in Warsaw ghetto.
Oct.	4	All Jews in German concentration camps ordered deported to Auschwitz.
Dec.	17	Allied nations pledge punishment for extermination of Jews.

1943

| Jan. | 18 | Warsaw-ghetto Jews launch first civilian armed resistance to Nazis: four days of street fighting. |

Apr.	19	At Bermuda conference, U.S. and British delegates fail to produce plans for saving Nazi victims.
Feb.	2	German Sixth Army surrenders at Stalingrad: turning point of war.
Mar.		Transports to death camps increase from many parts of Nazi-occupied Europe.
	13	New crematoriums open in Auschwitz.
Apr.	19	Warsaw Ghetto Uprising begins.
June	11	Deportation of Jews from Polish ghettos to death camps ordered. Deportations extended to Soviet ghettos.
Aug.		Russian army captures Kharkov. Revolt in Bialystok ghetto. Inmates revolt in Treblinka death camp.
Oct.	1	Expulsion of Danish Jews ordered: Danish underground rescues 7,000; only 475 captured by Germans.
	14	Inmate uprising in Sobibor death camp.
	20	UN War Crimes Commission set up.

1944

June	6	D-Day: Allied invasion of Nazi-occupied Western Europe begins in Normandy, France.
July	20	Attempted assassination of Hitler fails.
	24	Russian troops liberate Maidanek death camp.
Aug.	6	SS begins to drive concentration-camp inmates back into interior of Germany, as advancing Soviet army threatens to free them.
	23	Paris liberated by Allies.
Oct.		Last gassings in Auschwitz.
	26	Himmler orders destruction of Auschwitz crematoriums, as Nazis try to hide evidence of death camps.

1945

Jan.	11	Soviet troops take Warsaw.
	17–26	Soviet troops liberate 80,000 Jews in Budapest; take Auschwitz, find a few thousand survivors.
Feb.	4	Allies in Yalta conference plan spheres of influence for postwar Europe.
Apr.	11–28	U.S. troops liberate Buchenwald and Dachau. British troops liberate Belsen concentration camp. Soviet

troops reach outskirts of Berlin. Nazis evacuate prisoners from Sachsenhausen and Ravensbruck camps. SS commits last massacres.

	30	Hitler commits suicide in Berlin bunker.
May	2	Berlin surrenders.
	7	Germans surrender to Allies unconditionally.
Aug.	6	First atom bomb dropped by U.S. on Hiroshima, Japan.
	15	Japan surrenders: World War II ends.
Nov.	22	Nuremberg Trials of Nazi leaders begin.

BIBLIOGRAPHY

What crystallized the decision to write this book was a pamphlet by Henry Friedlander called *On the Holocaust: A Critique of the Treatment of the Holocaust in History Textbooks.** (Professor Friedlander, a German Jew, was eleven years old when the Nazis deported him to the Lodz ghetto and from there to Auschwitz.) A study of American high school textbooks, he said, showed that "their treatment of Nazism was brief, bland, superficial, and misleading." Racism, anti-Semitism, and the Holocaust were either ignored or dismissed in a few lines. History textbooks designed for the colleges and universities were "not substantially better." He quotes the anti-Nazi historian Golo Mann: "Darkness hides the vilest crime ever perpetrated by man against man."

Beyond the bounds of the traditional textbook there is a large literature on many aspects of the Holocaust. A bibliography of those studies is available in English, prepared by Jacob Robinson: *The Holocaust and After: Sources and Literature in English,* Israel Universities Press, Jerusalem, 1973. It includes books, articles, films, plays, television productions, and even reviews of books. The 353 pages contain 6,637 entries.

My purpose was to write a short book, a book that could be read by young and old, by people who know little or nothing about the Holocaust. I have tried to provide enough historical background to make its place in time clear. The military aspects of the war it is linked to are only touched upon, nor is there much detail on the inner politics of the Nazi regime or the international politics which are inseparable from the event.

My focus is the human experience: what happened to the Jews of Europe, what it meant to them, and what it means for all the rest of us, Jews and non-Jews alike. This is told in their own words as much as possible. There is no attempt to be comprehensive. A book of this kind can only suggest the nature of what many agree is the most significant and terrible event of the twentieth century.

* Anti-Defamation League of B'nai B'rith, New York, 1973.

For those who want to read more, there are now several large-scale histories of the Holocaust. The newest is by Lucy Dawidowicz: *The War Against the Jews 1933–1945*. The others, also listed in the history section of this bibliography, are by Hilberg, Levin, Manvell, Poliakov, and Reitlinger.

The titles in my bibliography are chiefly those I made use of myself. They are presented under various headings somewhat arbitrarily, in order to help readers find the material of their special concern. Obviously, there is considerable overlapping; the divisions are not rigid. I have omitted references to articles in historical journals, especially the many I drew from in the *Yivo Annual of Jewish Social Science*. Nor do I include important literary materials—novels, stories, poems, plays—or what can be found in the nonprint media—films, filmstrips, slides, tapes, exhibits, recordings. Lists of such material can be obtained from the American Association for Jewish Education, 114 Fifth Avenue, New York, N.Y. 10011.

A final word on the oral history of the Holocaust. A number of institutions here and abroad are conducting oral history programs on the Holocaust. They are taping and transcribing interviews with survivors and, sometimes, with the next generation as well. The largest such collection is at the Yad Vashem Institute in Jerusalem.

Anti-Semitism

*Arendt, Hannah, *The Origins of Totalitarianism*. Cleveland: The World Publishing Company, 1958.

Cohn, Norman, *Warrant for Genocide: The Myth of the Jewish World-Conspiracy and the Protocols of the Elders of Zion*. New York: Harper & Row, Publishers, Inc., 1969.

Davies, Alan T., *Anti-Semitism and the Christian Mind: The Crisis of Conscience After Auschwitz*. New York: Herder & Herder, 1969.

*Flannery, Edward H., *Anguish of the Jews: Twenty-Three Centuries of Anti-Semitism*. New York: The Macmillan Company, 1965.

Littell, Franklin, *The Crucifixion of the Jews*. New York: Harper & Row, Publishers, Inc., 1975.

*Mosse, George L., *Germans and Jews: The Right, the Left, and the Search for a "Third Force" in Pre-Nazi Germany*. New York: Howard Fertig, Inc., 1970.

Poliakov, Leon, *The Aryan Myth*. New York: Basic Books, Inc., Publishers, 1974.

* Available in paperback.

Samuel, Maurice, *The Great Hatred*. New York: Alfred A. Knopf, Inc., 1948.

*Schweitzer, Frederick M., *A History of the Jew Since the First Century A.D.* New York: The Macmillan Company, 1971.

Weinreich, Max, *Hitler's Professors*. New York: YIVO, 1946.

History

Dawidowicz, Lucy S., *The War Against the Jews 1933–1945*. New York: Holt, Rinehart and Winston, Inc., 1975.

Fisher, Julius S., *Transnistria: The Forgotten Cemetery*. New York: A. S. Barnes & Co., Inc., Yoseloff, 1969.

Fishman, Joshua R., ed., *Studies on Polish Jewry, 1919–1939*. New York: YIVO, 1974.

*Hilberg, Raul, *The Destruction of the European Jews*. New York: Quadrangle/The New York Times Book Co., 1961.

*————, ed., *Documents of Destruction*. New York: Quadrangle/The New York Times Book Co., 1971.

*Hitler, Adolf, *Mein Kampf*. Boston: Houghton Mifflin Company, 1943.

*Jarman, T. L., *The Rise and Fall of Nazi Germany*. New York: New York University Press, 1956.

Katz, Robert, *Black Sabbath: A Journey Through a Crime Against Humanity*. New York: The Macmillan Company, 1969.

*Kogon, Eugen, *The Theory and Practice of Hell: The German Concentration Camps and the System Behind Them*. New York: Octagon Books, Division of Farrar, Straus & Giroux, Inc.

*Levin, Nora, *The Holocaust: The Destruction of European Jewry, 1933–1945*. New York: T. Y. Crowell Co., 1968.

Levy, Claud, and Tillard, Paul, *Betrayal at the Vel D'Hiv*. New York: Hill & Wang, 1969.

Manvell, Roger, and Fraenkel, Heinrich, *The Incomparable Crime: Mass Extermination in the Twentieth Century: The Legacy of Guilt*. New York: G. P. Putnam's Sons, 1967.

Pilch, Judah, ed., *The Jewish Catastrophe in Europe*. New York: American Association for Jewish Education, 1968.

Poliakov, Leon, *Harvest of Hate: The Nazi Program for the Destruction of the Jews of Europe*. Westport, Conn.: Greenwood Press, Inc., 1971.

Presser, Jacob, *The Destruction of the Dutch Jews*. New York: E. P. Dutton & Co., Inc., 1969.

*Reitlinger, Gerald, *The Final Solution: The Attempt to Exterminate* the Jews of Europe, 1939–1945. New York: A. S. Barnes & Co., Inc., 1961.

*Schoenberner, Gerhard, The Yellow Star: The Persecution of the Jews in Europe, 1933–1945. New York: Bantam Books, Inc., 1973.

The Nazi Regime

*Allen, William Sheridan, The Nazi Seizure of Power: The Experience of a Single German Town, 1930–1935. New York: Franklin Watts, Inc., 1965.

*Bullock, Alan, Hitler: A Study in Tyranny. New York: Harper & Row, Publishers, Inc., 1964.

Dallin, Alexander, German Rule In Russia, 1941–1945: A Study of Occupation Policies. New York: St. Martin's Press, Inc., 1957.

*Heiden, Konrad, Der Fuehrer: Hitler's Rise to Power. Boston: Houghton Mifflin Company, 1944.

Merkl, Peter H., Political Violence Under the Swastika. Princeton: Princeton University Press, 1975.

*Neumann, Franz, Behemoth: The Structure and Practice of National Socialism. New York: Harper & Row, Publishers, Inc., 1966.

Noakes, Jeremy, and Pridham, Geoffrey, Documents on Nazism, 1919–1945. New York: The Viking Press, Inc., 1974.

Reitlinger, Gerald, The S.S.: Alibi of a Nation, 1922–1945. New York: The Viking Press, Inc., 1957.

*Schoenbaum, David, Hitler's Social Revolution: Class and Status in Nazi Germany, 1933–1939. New York: Doubleday & Co., Inc., 1967.

Stern, J. P., Hitler: The Fuehrer and the People. Berkeley: University of California Press, 1975.

*Trevor-Roper, Hugh R., The Last Days of Hitler. New York: The Macmillan Company, Collier Books, 1966.

Personal Accounts

Cohen, Elie A., The Abyss: A Confession. New York: W. W. Norton & Company, Inc., 1973.

Donat, Alexander, The Holocaust Kingdom: A Memoir. New York: Holt, Rinehart and Winston, Inc., 1969.

*Frank, Anne, The Diary of Anne Frank. New York: Pocket Books, 1971.

Frankl, Viktor E., *From Death-Camp to Existentialism: A Psychiatrist's Path to a New Therapy*. Boston: Beacon Press, Inc., 1959.

*Goldstein, Bernard, *The Stars Bear Witness*. New York: The Viking Press, Inc., 1949.

*Goldstein, Charles, *The Bunker*. New York: Atheneum Publishers, 1970.

Hart, Kitty. *I am Alive*. London: Abelard-Schuman, Ltd., 1961.

Heimler, Eugene, *Concentration Camp*. New York: Pyramid Communications, Inc., 1961.

Kantor, Alfred, *The Book of Alfred Kantor*. New York: McGraw-Hill, Inc., 1971.

*Katsh, Abraham, ed., *The Warsaw Diary of Chaim A. Kaplan*. New York: The Macmillan Company. Collier Books, 1973.

Kruk, Herman, *Diary of the Vilno Ghetto*. New York: YIVO, 1961.

Lengyel, Olga, *Five Chimneys: The Story of Auschwitz*. Chicago: Ziff Davis Publishing Co., 1947.

*Levi, Primo, *Survival in Auschwitz: The Nazi Assault on Humanity*. New York: The Macmillan Company, Collier Books, 1961.

Lind, Jacov, *Counting My Steps: An Autobiography*. New York: The Macmillan Company, 1969.

Meed, Vladka, *On Both Sides of the Wall: Memoirs from the Warsaw Ghetto*. Israel: Ghetto Fighters' House and Hakibbutz Hameuchad Publishing House, 1972.

*Nyiszli, Miklos, *Auschwitz: A Doctor's Eyewitness Account*. New York: Frederick Fell, Inc., 1960.

*Ringelblum, Emmanuel, *Notes from the Warsaw Ghetto: The Journal of Emmanuel Ringelblum*. New York: McGraw-Hill, Inc., 1958.

Shapell, Nathan, *Witness to the Truth*. New York: David McKay Co., Inc., 1974.

Wells, Leon W., *The Janowska Road*. New York: The Macmillan Company, 1963.

*Wiesel, Elie, *Night*. New York: Hill & Wang, 1960.

The Judenrat

Trunk, Isaiah, *Judenrat: The Jewish Councils in Eastern Europe under Nazi Occupation*. New York: The Macmillan Company, 1972.

Tushnet, Leonard, *The Pavement of Hell: 3 Leaders of the Judenrat*. New York: St. Martin's Press, Inc., 1972.

Yivo, *Imposed Jewish Governing Bodies Under Nazi Rule*. New York: YIVO Institute for Jewish Research, 1972.

Resistance

Ainsztein, Reuben, *Jewish Resistance in Nazi-Occupied Eastern Europe, with a Historical Survey of the Jew as a Fighter and Soldier in the Diaspora*. New York: Barnes & Noble, Inc., 1974.

*Bauer, Yehuda, *They Chose Life: Jewish Resistance in the Holocaust*. New York: The American Jewish Committee, 1973.

Donat, Alexander, *Jewish Resistance*. New York: Warsaw Ghetto Resistance Organization, 1964.

*Elkins, Michael, *Forged in Fury*. New York: Ballantine Books, Inc., 1971.

Friedman, Philip, *Their Brothers' Keepers*. New York: Crown Publishers, Inc., 1957.

Horbach, Michael, *Out of the Night*. New York: Frederick Fell, Inc., 1967.

Kimche, John and David, *The Secret Roads: The "Illegal" Migration of a People, 1938–1948*. London: Secker & Warburg, 1954.

Mark, Ber, *Uprising in the Warsaw Ghetto*. New York: Schocken Books, Inc., 1975.

Michel, Henri, *The Shadow War: Resistance in Europe 1939–1945*. New York: Harper & Row, Publishers, Inc., 1973.

*Suhl, Yuri, ed., *They Fought Back: The Story of the Jewish Resistance in Nazi Europe*. New York: Crown Publishers, Inc., 1967.

Refugees and World Response

Bauer, Yehuda, *Flight and Rescue: Brichah*. New York: Random House, Inc., 1970.

Feingold, Henry L., *The Politics of Rescue: the Roosevelt Administration and the Holocaust, 1938–1945*. New Brunswick, N.J.: Rutgers University Press, 1970.

*Flender, Harold, *Rescue in Denmark*. New York: Simon & Schuster, Inc., 1963.

Friedman, Saul S., *No Haven for the Oppressed: United States Policy Toward Jewish Refugees, 1933–1945*. Detroit: Wayne State University Press, 1973.

*Morse, Arthur D., *While Six Million Died: A Chronicle of American Apathy*. New York: Random House, Inc., 1967.

Postwar Trials

*Arendt, Hannah, *Eichmann in Jerusalem: A Report on the Banality of Evil*. New York: The Viking Press, Inc., 1964.

Hausner, Gideon, *Justice in Jerusalem*. New York: Harper & Row, Publishers, Inc., 1966.

Robinson, Jacob, *And the Crooked Shall be Made Straight: The Eichmann Trial, the Jewish Catastrophe, and Hannah Arendt's Narrative*. New York: The Macmillan Company, 1965.

*Wiesenthal, Simon, *The Murderers Among Us*. New York: McGraw-Hill, Inc., 1967.

Anthologies

Friedlander, Albert H., *Out of the Whirlwind: A Reader of Holocaust Literature*. New York: Union of American Hebrew Congregations, 1968.

*Glatstein, Jacob; Knox, Israel; and Margoshes, Samuel, eds., *Anthology of Holocaust Literature*. New York: Jewish Publication Society of America, 1969.

Halperin, Irving, *Messengers From the Dead: Literature of the Holocaust*. Philadelphia: The Westminster Press, 1970.

Korman, Gerd, ed., *Hunter and Hunted: Human History of the Holocaust*. New York: The Viking Press, Inc., 1973.

Search for Meaning

Berkovitz, Eliezer, *Faith After the Holocaust*. New York: KTAV Publishing House, Inc., 1973.

Borowitz, Eugene. *How Can a Jew Speak of Faith Today*. Philadelphia: The Westminster Press, 1969.

Cohen, Arthur A., *Arguments and Doctrines: A Reader of Jewish Thinking in the Aftermath of the Holocaust*. New York: Harper & Row, Publishers, Inc., 1970.

*Fackenheim, Emil L., *God's Presence in History: Jewish Affirmation and Philosophic Reflections*. New York: Harper & Row, Publishers, Inc., 1972.

*Rubenstein, Richard L., *After Auschwitz: Radical Theology and Contemporary Judaism*. Indianapolis: The Bobbs-Merrill Co., Inc., 1966.

*Wiesel, Elie, *One Generation After*. New York: Random House, Inc., 1970.

INDEX

Ainsztein, Reuben, 143
American Joint Distribution Committee, 44, 102, 187
Anielewicz, Mordecai, 162
anti-Jewish legislation, 33–41
anti-Semitism, xii, 43, 201; under czarism, 60–61; link to extermination, 107; Hitler's use of, 15; mobilizes Germans for war, 39; Nazi development of, 16, 32–34; in Poland, 61, 62, 185, 187; in pre-Hitler Germany, 6–9; roots of, 3
Arabs: allied to Hitler, 46; invade Israel, 187; and Palestine partition, 187
Arendt, Hannah, 138
Armenians, massacre of, 192
Arndt, Rudi, 151
Artur, Z., 63
Aryanism, 7
assimilation, 32, 61–62
Atlas, Ezekial, 168
Auschwitz camp, 33, 89, 91, 106, 107, 114, 117, 127, 130, 131, 132; crematoriums blown up in, 182, 183, 184, 192, 197, 199, 201; escapes from, 178–179; eyewitness reports on, 118–126, 179; revolt in, 178–181
Austria, Nazi annexation of, 43, 59; Jews in, 43

Babi Yar, 65
badge, Jewish, 4
Baeck, Leo, 38
Baermann, Hans, 92–93
Ball-Kaduri, K. J., 29
Barash, Ephraim, 83
Baum group, 150–153
Baum, Herbert, 150–153
Baum, Marianne, 150–153
Belzec camp, 107, 127, 128–130, 186, 199
Bialik, Chaim N., 98
Bialystok ghetto, 83, 107, 164–166, 199
Bielski brothers, 167
Birkenau camp, 140
Bismarck, Otto von, 7–8, 11
Blaskowitz, Johannes, 65
book burning, 20–21
Bot, Salek, 171
boycotts, 34, 195

Bradfisch, Otto, 64
Buch, Walter, 54
Buchenwald camp, 28, 138, 151, 182–183, 196; revolt in, 183, 199
Bund, Jewish Labor, 62, 63, 100, 109, 110, 111, 114, 115, 157

camps. See concentration camps, death camps, labor camps, names of individual camps
Catholic Center, 18, 20
Catholic Church, Jews and, 3–5, 54–55, 60, 127–128, 131
Chamberlain, Houston S., 8, 10
Chamberlain, Neville, 44
Chelmno camp, 106, 107, 198
children: in Auschwitz, 122; in Baum group, 149–153; beaten at school, 35–36; bound for Israel, 184–185; deported from France, 114; deported from orphanage, 112–113; in forced labor, 90–93; in French resistance, 158; in Hitler Youth, 39; in ghettos, 85–87; made informers, 22–24; murdered by killing squads, 66–70; poem by, 103; as saboteurs, 174–175; in secret schools, 99–100; in underground, 137–138
Chorazyski, Julian, 175
Christianity, Jews and, 3–6, 30, 153

Christian Social Workers' party, 8
collaboration, 145–147
Communists, 18, 19, 20, 28, 151, 166
concentration camps, 26, 27–30
conversion to Christianity, 32
Cracow ghetto, 78, 100, 107, 163
Crusades, x, 4
Cuker, Golda, 157–158
Czechoslovakia: subjugation of, 44, 59, 196, 197; Jews in, 44
Czerniakow, Adam, 146
Czernowitz ghetto, 79
Czestochowa, 90

Dabrowa, 144
Dachau camp, 28, 55, 131, 174, 195, 199
Dawidowicz, Lucy, 58–59, 202
death camps, Jewish losses in, 117, 178. See names of individual camps
Deblin, 90
deportations of Jews, 96, 98, 108, 162; from Austria, 117, 197; from Belgium, 117; from Czechoslovakia, 107, 117, 197; from France, 113, 117, 123, 133; from Galicia, 107; from Germany, 108, 117, 152, 198; from Greece, 117, 124–125; from Holland, 107, 117, 197; from Hungary, 117, 130; from Italy, 117, 121; from Lithuania, 153; from Yugoslavia, 117

Jewish police in, 84; mortality in, 80; as productive units, 93–94, 161; revolts in, 153, 161–169, 199; schools in, 99–100, 150; work in, 83; worship in, 101, 150. *See also* names of ghettos

Gobineau, Arthur de, 8, 10

Goebbels, Joseph, 19, 20–21, 22, 25, 33, 152, 163

Goering, Hermann, 19, 22, 25, 56, 77, 89, 106, 196, 198

Goldstein, Bernard, 97, 109

Graebe, Hermann, 70–73

Greenstein, Jacob, 137–138

Grynszpan, Herschel, 51, 196

Gypsies, 28, 132

Hasidim, 101, 144, 150

Heine, Heinrich, 21

Hess, Rudolf, 25

Heydrich, Reinhard, 27, 43, 44, 57, 59, 64, 65, 77, 106, 107, 198

High Commission for Refugees from Germany, 43

Hilberg, Raul, 16, 64, 130, 141, 142, 143

Himmler, Heinrich, 22, 25, 26, 27, 41, 77, 90, 130, 131, 162, 178, 199

Hindenburg, Paul von, 18, 19, 21, 195

Hirszfeld, Ludwik, 85–86

Hitler, Adolf, ix, x, xi, 3, 4, 5, 8, 9; aids France, 43; annexes Austria, 43, 196; becomes Chancellor, 18; becomes dictator, 20; begins terror against Jews, 31, 33–47; begins World War II, 58, 197; biography, 10–18; commits suicide, 182, 200; consolidates power, 19–22; destroys synagogues, 43; policy of expulsion, 42–45; invades Soviet Union, 65, 151, 198; and Nuremberg Laws, 36–38; as orator, 13–14; plot against, 199; remilitarizes Rhineland, 42, 196; subjugates Czechoslovakia, 44, 196; threatens extermination of Jews, 58, 64, 105, 197; use of coercion, 26; views on Jews, 11, 13, 15, 58

Hitler Youth, 22, 39–40

Holocaust: death toll in, xi, 190; defined, xi; ignored in textbooks, 201; pattern of, 33; the significance of, 191–193

"*Horst Wessel Lied*," 34

Höss, Rudolf, 130

hunger, 80, 111

Israel, 184, 187, 189

Jaspers, Karl, 192

Jehovah's Witnesses, 28, 29, 140

Jewish Councils (*Judenrat*), 60, 78, 82, 88, 153, 154, 197; and collaboration, 147; under czarism, 146–147; fate of, 146; functions of, 78–79, 83, 109; and resistance movements, 145–147

Peretz, Aaron, 86–87
Pinkas, Oscar, 96–97
poems, 98, 99, 100, 103
pogroms, x, 54, 56, 60–61, 63, 185, 197
Poliakov, Leon, 169
Popovicz, Traian, 79
population, Jewish: of Austria, 43; of Eastern Europe, 60; of Europe, 107; of Germany, 31, 35; of Israel, 187; of Poland, 59, 187; of Soviet Union, 65; of United States, 45; of Warsaw, 77, 114, 162
Protestant churches, Jews and, 5, 54–55

Rabinowicz, Chaim, 146
racism: and anti-feminism, 26; doctrine of, xi–xii, 73, 201; against Jews, 59, 61, 73; against Poles, 59
Rajzman, Samuel, 177
Rath, Ernst vom, 51, 56
Ravensbruck camp, 28, 131, 199
Rayman, Marcel, 171, 172
Red Cross, 89, 186
refugees. See emigration
Reich Association of Jews in Germany, 56
Reichstag fire, 19, 195
Representative Council of Jews in Germany, 38, 56
resistance, Jewish, 137–181, 197, 198; active, 109, 111, 158; armed and unarmed, 158, 161; in Belgium, 159; in Berlin, 150–153; condi-

tions of, 144–145, 147–148; in death camps, 174–181; degree of, 139, 141; in the Diaspora, 142–143; forms of, 140–141, 143–144, 153–159; in France, 148, 158–159, 170–172; in Holland, 138; and Jewish Councils, 145–147; led by youth, 148, 150–153, 161–164; passive, 98, 143, 150, 158; in Russia, 137–138; by women, 165, 168–169, 170, 179–181
Rhineland, remilitarized, 42, 59, 196
Riga ghetto, 92, 108–109, 138
Ringelblum, Emmanuel, 84–85, 93, 95, 98, 101–102, 104, 147, 197
Ritter, Karl, 172
Robinson, Jacob, 201
Robota, Rosa, 179–181
Roechling, 89
Roehm, Ernst, 21
Rome-Berlin Axis, 196
Roosevelt, Franklin D., Jewish refugees and, 43, 45
Rosenberg, Reuben, 90–91
Rosenberg, Walter, 179
Rosin, Arnost, 179
Rothholz, Lotte, 152–153

SA (Storm Troopers), 21, 34
sabotage, 141, 152, 153–154, 158, 159
Sachsenhausen camp, 28, 29, 199
St. Louis (ship), 46–47
Salaspils camp, 92

Warsaw Ghetto Uprising, 141, 147, 162–164, 175, 198, 199

Weidemann, *Landesbischof*, 55

Weimar Republic, 12, 13, 32

Weizmann, Chaim, 42

Wellers, Georges, 114

Wetzler, Alfred, 179

Wiesel, Elie, 138–139, 182–183

Wiesenthal, Simon, 186

Wilhelm II, 11

Wittenberg, Itzik, 145

Wladka, Feigele, 111

Wolf, Jeanette, 108–109

women: as deportees, 108–109; position under Nazis, 25–26; in resistance, 81, 157–158, 165, 168–169, 179–181

World War I, 11–13, 31, 40, 44, 61, 96

World War II, 46, 58, 131, 197, 200

Yad Vashem, 141

Yivo Institute for Jewish Research, 141–142

Yosselevscka, Rivka, 66–70

youth, under Nazism, 22–24

Zabladowicz, Noah, 179–181

Zimmerman, Hersz, 171

Zionists, 62, 101, 102, 110, 114, 151, 162, 164, 179, 184–185

Zygelbojm, Shmuel, 115

Zyklon B gas, 127

Format by Kohar Alexanian
Set in 11 pt. Electra
Composed by American Book–Stratford Press, Inc.
Printed and bound by The Murray Printing Company
HARPER & ROW, PUBLISHERS, INCORPORATED

MAP OF EUROPE SHOWING CAMP AREA

North
Sea

Baltic Sea

Atlantic
Ocean

Mediterranean Sea

Copenhagen

North Sea

Hamburg

NEUENGAMME

Bremen

PAPENBURG

RAVENSBRUCK

SACHSENHAUSEN

BERGEN-BELSEN

Amsterdam

Berlin

DORANORDHAUSEN

Leipzig

BUCHENWALD

Frankfurt

THERESIENSTADT

FLOSSENBÜRG

Nuremberg

NATZVILLER

DACHAU

LANDSBERG

Munich

MAUTHAUSEN

Zurich

Bern

X Extermination Camps
● Concentration Camps
• Towns